CU00404598

The New Green Juicing Diet

With 60+ Alkalizing, Energizing, Detoxifying, Fat Burning Recipes

Elizabeth Swann

FASTLANE PUBLISHING

The New Green Juicing Diet: With 60+ Alkalizing, Energizing, Detoxifying, Fat Burning Recipes
by Elizabeth Swann Miller

Copyright 2013 by Elizabeth Swann
All Rights Reserved

Copyright Notice: This book was published by Ari Freidman under Fast Lane Publishing. No part of this publication may be reproduced in any form or by any means including scanning, photocopying or otherwise without prior written permission of the copyright holder.

The information provided in this book is designed to provide helpful information on the subjects discussed. This book is not meant to be used, nor should it be used, to diagnose or treat any medical condition. For diagnosis or treatment of any medical problem, consult your own physician.

The publisher and author are not responsible for any specific health or allergy needs that may require medical supervision and are not liable for any damages or negative consequences from any treatment, action, application or preparation, to any person reading or following the information in this book.

References are provided for informational purposes only and do not constitute endorsement of any websites or other sources. Readers should be aware that the websites listed in this book may change.

If you would like to do any of the above, please contact us for permission at:
Contact@fastlanepublishing.com

ISBN: 978-965-7636-01-5

Printed In The United States of America

Contents

Also by Elizabeth Swann (Miller)

The New Green Smoothie Diet Solution

Pure Green

3 Day Green Smoothie Detox

Introduction

Maybe you've picked up this green juicing book because you feel tired and depleted. Even after sleeping for a full eight hours each night, you feel exhausted when you wake up in the morning– as if sleeping itself was a chore. Maybe you are reading this green juicing book because you are overweight and all the diet programs you have tried have failed, miserably, leaving you hungry and yes, tired again. Perhaps you are suffering from stress on a pretty consistent basis and feel like every day is just another day to get through, instead of knowing joyfulness and a certain joie de vivre that life can offer.

You may remember a time when you were more exuberant and really desire recapturing that feeling. Are you sick and tired of feeling *sick and tired*? Maybe you decided to read this book because you have a gut instinct that you could feel less run-down and could even boost your overall health to optimum levels with green juicing.

My name is Liz. I turned to green juicing because I was facing some pretty serious health issues including high cholesterol and obesity. Through what I learned while enrolled in a four-year curriculum to transform myself into a licensed naturopath, I came to know how to green juice my way to a completely new body and mind. I feel fantastic every day now and I am absolutely thrilled to share all that I know about green juicing, both through the books I write, and through the act of treating others in my private practice. As you're about to learn, green juices treat problems at their roots rather than simply working to alleviate symptoms.

The fact that you picked up this book means *you* are willing to listen, and I am so glad, because green juicing really can save your life, and restore a younger, more energetic and fun-filled version of yourself that you may forgotten even existed. I promise you – she or he is still in there, and I am going to help you chisel away at the tired, bored, apathetic, run down version of you with green juicing fun until you rediscover a healthy, happy, excited-about-every-day person that is lurking underneath a rundown body and exhausted mind.

By the time you finish reading this book, and putting these fun, easy green-juicing techniques into action, you will have more energy, clear skin, sleep like a baby, and look and feel terrific!

Your Green Juicing Adventure Begins Here!

I want you to see green juicing as a way to rediscover your more adventurous self. In the words of Whitney Ferre, *"Everyone has a choice to see life as a to-do list or a journey. The first leads to 'work' and the second leads to 'adventure'. Which do you choose?"*

You see, green juicing shouldn't be another thing you have to do, but a great adventure you embark on. Just think of all you are about to learn about your health and wellbeing and how to restore it, as well as all the great green juicing recipes you'll discover.

Green juice also tastes great, and even though those strange green concoctions don't *look* like they taste great, you often can't even taste the green in them! For example, when you cook spinach it has a very distinctive flavor, but when you blend it with apple juice, you get all the same nutritional benefits, only you mostly just taste the sweetness of apples.

You can get more energy from a 6-ounce glass of green juice than you can by guzzling down a 16-ounce cup of coffee from a drive through in the morning. Green juices are also full of B vitamins, so you won't feel like you 'need another hit' of caffeine half way through your day in order to make it to five o'clock. B vitamins supply sustained energy that lasts, without causing spikes in energy followed by a big let down like you've been on some kind of energetic roller coaster.

You can also look forward to going to the bathroom more regularly, and not feeling constipated anymore since green juices are full of fiber and enzymes as well as nutrients that help keep your digestive system running like clockwork. In some healing traditions, all disease is considered to start in the gut, so flushing nasty toxins out of your system will help prevent disease while also keeping you looking and feeling absolutely divine.

I talked a little bit about my health problems; but they were just one reason I wanted to start green juicing. I had a difficult relationship with food, I was exhausted, and I felt weak. Even though I was about to get married and though I was looking forward to my new life, I just couldn't seem to break the vicious cycle of stress followed by binges on sweet, fried, or salty comfort foods. When I learned about the benefits that come with eliminating processed foods, gluten, and dairy products, I decided to eliminate them from my diet. I am thankful every day for how I feel now that I've been doing it for a while.

Finally, I'd also like to say congratulations on your decision to purchase this book. Doing so is the *first step* in making positive, long-lasting changes in your lifestyle and eating habits so that you can live life that way it's meant to be lived, passionately.

How to Get the Most from This Book

We'll start with a quick introduction, where you'll learn exactly what green juicing is and how it differs from regular juicing or smoothie making. You'll also learn how to make lots of different types of green juices and learn what each kind of fruit or vegetable adds to your green juice as far as their health benefits. There will be over **60 different juicing recipes** to choose from!

You can flip through this book to the section that interests you, for instance, if you want recipes for detoxing, or losing weight, or for more beauty and vitality. Alternatively, you can read the book from start to finish and learn everything you could ever want to know about green juicing.

Note from Liz: A quick word about the recipes in this book. All 60+ recipes are 100% raw, preservative and lactose free which makes them perfect for anyone following a strictly vegan or raw food diet. These flavor packed recipes were created with over 10 years of experience in juicing to ensure ease of use, maximum taste, absorption and health benefits. So I hope you enjoy drinking them and experience their many amazing health benefits!

You'll easily be able to access the recipes by referring to the table of contents and searching the recipes by health benefit.

Here's a quick breakdown of what you will learn in each chapter:

- ↻ **Why Green Juice?** This chapter covers all you need to know about why you should use green juices and smoothies for better health, and a million other amazing benefits. It also tells you *what* a green juice is. (The answer may surprise you). You will understand why you should green juice, even if you don't juice solely, as a means to the most audaciously wonderful version of yourself ever. Don't think good health, think, super-human health!

⮑ **Why Greens?** In this chapter we will cover what exactly it does for your body, mind and spirit to drink your greens instead of just eat them, and how green juicing specifically can drastically overhaul your health. You're going to look and feel fantastic!

⮑ **Alkalizing Energy** in this chapter we will discuss what body pH is and why you need an alkaline environment in your body in order to experience peak health levels. Green juicing is one of the best ways to get alkaline fast and stay that way.

⮑ **How to Create the Perfect Green Juice** Even though you will end up making some of your own fabulous creations after you have had some practice, all on your own, this chapter will discuss exactly how to prepare, and consume green juices. It's as easy as 1,2,3 with our list of the best ways to make a delicious green juice starting today.

⮑ **Storing Green Juices At Home and on the Go.** goes over the ever-important process of storing your green juices so they stay packed full of nutrition and don't spoil in your refrigerator or when you take them to go.

⮑ **How to Combine Greens, Fruits, and Other Ingredients for taste and health benefits.** This chapter will unveil the secrets of combining ingredients for a taste-bud treat and some out of this world health benefits. It will also discuss ratios and amounts.

⮑ **Prepping Your Ingredients for the Best Green Juices.** If you don't prep your vegetables and fruits properly, you can miss out on some of the benefits of green juicing. This chapter covers all you need to know to get it right from the start.

⮑ **Let's Get a Juicer.** You won't want to continue juicing if you have a lousy juicer. In this chapter you will learn three possibilities in a low, medium, and higher price range, so that you can have the best equipment to juice right.

⮑ **Taking Care of Your Green Juicing Equipment.** If you invest in a juicer, no matter its price-level, you want it to last, and keep it clean so that you don't contaminate the items you will be juicing. This chapter gives you tips and tricks to make your juicer last as long as possible.

- **Easing into Green Juicing.** I know you haven't been chugging the green since you were just out of your mother's womb, but hopefully you will make this a life-long habit by starting slow and sticking to it. I'll tell you how.

- **How to Create a daily juicing habit Once you start, don't stop.** I will show you how to keep the healthy habit of green juicing going.

- **How to Prepare a Weekly Shopping List.** Learn exactly what you need to do to keep a green juicing habit going. It all starts in the grocery store, or if you're lucky enough, in your own organic garden.

- **Going Organic.** This chapter will discuss why organic fruits and vegetables are so vital as well as the cautions and side effects of juicing.

- **How to Green Juice on a Budget.** Many people mistakenly think that green juicing is too expensive to develop a habit for it. This is simply not true. I'll show you how to keep green juicing on the cheap.

- **Green Juicing to Detoxify the Body.** In this section we will get down to the nitty-gritty about why it is so important to cleanse the body's organs and detoxify with green juicing.

- **Green Juicing For Weight Loss.** Here you will learn how easy it is to lose weight with green juicing, kill sugar cravings for good, and supplement solid foods in the event you want to replace an entire meal with a green juice. You will also learn how to achieve amazing results with the great tasting recipes for delicious green juices that will supercharge your weight loss goals.

- **Green Juicing to Fight the Negative Effects of Stress.** In this section you will learn just how damaging stress is and exactly what green juicing does to reduce its horrific effects on your body, mind, and over all well-being.

- **Green Juicing for Amazing Energy.** Here you will learn how to boost your energy pre-and post-workout, or just to get through a demanding day. You don't need to count on caffeine, or energy drinks, which are really bad for you. Green juice to the rescue!

- **Green Juicing to Boost Brain Power.** If you only knew how much more alert, attentive and relaxed your brain could be on a regular basis with green juicing, you'd start and never stop. You'll find out just why green juicing is the ultimate brain boosting practice.

- **Green Juicing to Strengthen the Immune System.** In this section you'll learn exactly what green juicing can do to make your body a disease-fighting powerhouse. Say goodbye to numerous illnesses and even the common cold with green juicing.

- **Green Juicing for Beauty.** If you want glowing skin and luxurious hair without spending tons of money on spa treatments and facials, endless hair shampoos and conditioners, then green juice. You'll learn exactly how green juices are better than Ponce De Leon's fountain of youth.

- **Adding and Extra Kick to Your Green Juices.** Here you will learn how to add some interesting and easily available extra ingredients to your green juices and smoothies to make them even more amazing and nutrient-packed.

- **FAQ's on Green Juicing.** We'll cover 10 of the most commonly asked questions about green juicing for maximum benefits and troubleshooting.

- **Your Super Encyclopedia of Green Juice Ingredients** you will have access to a master list of greens, fruits, vegetables, and even additional mix-ins that can add some seriously astonishing health benefits to your body. Think of this chapter as your encyclopedia of green juicing. You'll end up knowing all the health benefits of each ingredient as well as how they taste, what exactly is in them, and why they work, whether they are a protein, vitamin, mineral or other compound which is really great for your body. You'll also learn about side effects (though they are minimal) and any ingredients you should avoid, and why.

Why Green Juicing is So Great

The 'What and Why' of Green Juicing

What Exactly is Green Juicing?

Green juicing is a method of separating the juice of a vegetable or fruit from the pulp and fiber. When you separate the juice from the fibrous material of the green vegetables, which are the primary ingredient (though we will talk about adding others) they go directly into the bloodstream without the body having to digest them. It's like getting a quick dose of super-nutrients, also called 'micro-nutrients.' Without enough micronutrients to remove waste, your cells become congested, DNA gets broken, and the body doesn't have the ability to repair itself. Eventually, without the huge doses of micronutrients that green juicing provides, you can get sick, or at best, feel really tired and cranky.

Good quality greens are essential to make great green juices and smoothies and either a juicer or blender, though a juicer is preferred because it will do a better job of extracting the juice from the vegetables.

When you flood your cells with the micronutrients in green juices, you will feel an instant boost of pure, natural energy. With prolonged green juicing you will notice all sorts of beneficial changes. Your skin will glow, you will lose weight, and you will feel less tired, just for starters.

Green juicing is going to change your life. It does so many beneficial things for us, by the time you learn about them all you might wonder why you hadn't started this great habit sooner!

So, exactly why does it work so well? When you finish reading this chapter you will understand the ins and outs of green juicing like an expert. You'll also discover more than 15 reasons why you should green juice!

Are you wondering just why people green juice? Take a look:

Just Some of the Reasons People Green Juice Are:

- ⮑ To repair a depleted immune system
- ⮑ It's easier to consume vast amounts of veggies with green juicing than just by eating salads all day
- ⮑ To reverse stomach ulcers
- ⮑ You can use vegetables you might not normally eat in a juice and get their nutritional benefits without having to taste them
- ⮑ Parents can make sure their kids get enough vital nutrients in green juicing instead of arguing over broccoli at the dinner table
- ⮑ To cleanse their kidneys, liver, and gastrointestinal tract for better health
- ⮑ To lose weight
- ⮑ To aid in quitting smoking
- ⮑ To clear up adult and adolescent acne
- ⮑ To purge environmental toxins that come from the air, water, and soil as well as the buildings we live in
- ⮑ To sleep better
- ⮑ Reduce belly bloat
- ⮑ To cure cancer
- ⮑ To replace amino acids after a taxing workout
- ⮑ To Increase IQ scores
- ⮑ To oxygenate the body with chlorophyll, the main ingredient of all green juices
- ⮑ To feel happier, and more positive
- ⮑ For increased vitamins and nutrient consumption that goes straight to the blood

stream

There are literally hundreds more reasons to green juice, and you will probably discover your own personal reasons to keep your green juicing habit going strong once you've started it. The changes you will notice in your body, mind and emotions will be profound, and they are long lasting.

Green juicing is so effective, in fact, that many models, celebrities, and professional athletes drink green juices as part of their health regime, and we all know they are under some of the worst scrutiny – with people expecting them to be energetic, and beautiful well past their 'prime.'

Many of them accomplish amazing results using green juices and a sound workout routine, including:

- Gwyneth Paltrow–Actress
- Kelly Slater – Nine Times Surfing World Champion
- Sanoe Lake – Surfer, Actor and Model
- Rajon Rondo – NBA player for Boston Celtics
- Mariano Rivera – Baseball Player, New York Yankees
- Alicia Silverstein–Actress
- Russell Simmons – Music Mogul and Actor
- Owen Wilson–Actor
- Nicole Richie–Actress
- Mark Teixeira – Baseball Player
- Blake Lively–Actress
- Edward Norton–Actor
- Kim Cattrall–Actress
- Colin Farrell–Actor
- Karolina Kurkova–Model
- Miranda Kerr–Model
- Alessandra Ambrosio–Model
- Crystal Renn – Model

The list goes on and on, and while famous people green juice, everyday people do too.

You can use green juicing as a way to augment your current eating program. It doesn't need to be a drastic change. You can start small and then go crazy with green juicing if you feel inclined. You can use green juicing today to start feeling more energized, sexier, and full of youthful vitality. With some great vegetables, a few easy mix-ins and some creative recipes, you'll be ready to conquer the world.

Green Juicing a Rainbow

Did you know that your refrigerator can be transformed into a medicine cabinet overflowing with goodness? Thing is, green juicing isn't just greens, though this is the primary color of the juice. Green juices contain a rainbow of flavors and foods, so that you can be your healthiest and most fabulous self.

Just one green juicing recipe could contain beets (the color red), carrots (the color orange), barley grass (the color green), ginger (the color yellow), dinosaur kale (the color blue), and purple bell peppers or eggplant (the color purple). You get the idea – green juices can provide a rainbow of colors and flavors with all the amazing antioxidants that each vegetable, or fruit offers (and that doesn't even include exciting mix-ins like cacao powder or maca root powder to give your green juices and even more of a nutritional boost).

So as you can see, green juice can provide a massive boost to both your health and your feeling of wellbeing. I know it has with me.

Green: Juice's Most Important Color

Aside from the vitamins and minerals in green juicing ingredients we use, there is a reason that we should ensure there are greens in every juice we make. That's because greens are full of one of the most important substances on earth: chlorophyll. The same thing that makes trees and plants a bright green color, and imbues our landscape with verdant hues of olive, jade, and emerald is what gives our body the incredible health and vitality that it so deserves.

Why Chlorophyll is King

Many people are not very aware of the benefits of drinking, instead of eating large quantities of chlorophyll. After all, do you really get the minimal seven servings of vegetables that you should have on a daily basis to make sure all your nutrition needs are met? Drinking green juices is a fast and easy way to get all that nutrition — then some!

Chlorophyll, one of the nutrients of green vegetables is so important to plants that it allows them to convert light into energy they can use to grow, flower and pollinate. In people, chlorophyll has similar benefits. In biochemistry, they call this process the primary photoreceptor pigment. *Green* is King! Chlorophyll is a actually reflected in a blue-green light spectrum range, but we see it as green.

Spinach, a super green food, for example, contains 300 to 600 milligrams per ounce of chlorophyll, whereas olives contain about 1/1000th as much. If you think of some of the healthiest foods on the planet – they are all green:

- Brussels Sprouts
- Kale
- Leaks
- Collard Greens
- Swiss Chard
- Green peas
- Romaine Lettuce
- Turnip Greens
- Wheat Grass
- Barley Grass
- Sea vegetables
- Parsley
- Cilantro
- Basil
- Broccoli
- Bell Peppers
- Asparagus
- Green Cabbage

Now imagine trying to eat large quantities of these life-affirming foods every day. You wouldn't be able to eat much of anything else. The fiber in them would fill you up after just a few servings. Instead, imagine eating ALL of these greens in one day, mixed into super green juices with other ingredients as well. You would have a veritable storehouse of nutrition packed into a few glasses of great green juices.

In addition to the specific phytonutrients, minerals and vitamins in each of these foods, they are packed full of chlorophyll. Only greens can give you more chlorophyll and only *green juicing* can really deliver when it comes to super-human health.

Chlorophyll and Your Health

There has been lots of research conducted on chlorophyll and our health. It affects us positively, all the way down to our DNA. That's' quite impressive! It can even repair damaged DNA. It has been shown to decrease the disease of cancer, especially liver and skin cancers, and can also retard the aging process.

Additional Vitamins & Minerals in Green Juices

Just getting high levels of chlorophyll is wonderful, but green juicing also provides a full alphabet soup of vitamins that you need to lose weight, feel beautiful, look amazing, and combat all sorts of diseases. For example:

- Juiced collard and beet greens are full of vitamin A. Vitamin A does everything from improve your eyesight to boost your immune system, regulate your genes and to help promote the creation of red blood cells in your body.

- Juiced broccoli and asparagus are full of the entire spectrum of B vitamins – called the B complex, including B6. Just this one B vitamin, also called pyridoxine, is responsible for many chemical reactions in the body and is essential for metabolizing food. It helps treat premenstrual symptoms, depression, fatigue, irritability, and brain functioning. Vitamin B2, called riboflavin is important for releasing energy from carbohydrates that you eat. We can juice bok choy and Brussels sprouts, peas, artichoke and asparagus to get our Vitamin B2. Vitamin B3 or niacin can help with the skin and nerves, as well as help with high blood pressure. We juice artichokes and okra for example, to get more of this great vitamin in our bloodstreams.

- Vitamin C is important for helping your immune system as well as detoxing the body from the effects of radiation. It was even used to effectively help the survivors of the recent Fukushima disaster. That's how important this one little vitamin is. It also helps the liver detox the body and reduces the incidence of cancer. And guess what – juiced parsley, broccoli, cauliflower, tomatoes, celery and spinach are full of vitamin C.

- Vitamin D is in all leafy green vegetables. This vitamin must be in balance in the body to create healthy bones, to regulate the immune system and to reduce inflammation. Spinach is a great vegetable to add to your green juices to get your vitamin D.

- Vitamin E and Folate are the skin beautifiers. Leafy greens come to the rescue again with loads of Vitamin E. Vitamin E also makes sure that your brain cells stay healthy and makes sure to keep 'bad' cholesterol down. Vitamin E is a powerful antioxidant that can prevent certain forms of cancer, too. Kale, collards, spinach and broccoli, are all full of vitamin E and folate.

- Vitamin F is found in juiced spirulina, sprouts, wheat germ and flaxseed and sunflower oils. This important, but lesser known vitamin is also known as a healthy fatty acid. Vitamin F is primarily derived from Omega 3 and Omega 6 fatty acids. These are key elements to a high-functioning brain, a great mood, balanced energy levels and even cancer prevention.

- ⮑ Vitamin K is also sometimes called the forgotten vitamin, but it is very important (along with vitamin D) to protect against cardiovascular disease, and loss of bone mass, which can lead to diseases like Osteoporosis. Vitamin K as also proven to reduce the chances of getting certain types of cancer and has been shown to reduce Alzheimer's symptoms as well as reduce someone's tendency to bruise too easily. Vitamin K is juiced in Brussels Sprouts, Cabbage, Green Beans, Chives, Collard Greens and Cilantro.

- ⮑ Trace Minerals in Green Juices

Another great reason to green juice is because it is one of the fastest ways to get a load of trace minerals that are so necessary for great health. Minerals are necessary for many reasons. Here are just a few:

- ⮑ They help to regulate our heartbeat.

- ⮑ Minerals build strong teeth and bones.

- ⮑ Minerals help to regulate our hormones – a very important thing to control weight and health.

- ⮑ Help our bodies grow and replenish old tissue and cells.

- ⮑ To transmit nerve impulses.

We can get trace minerals from numerous vegetables and fruits, and when we juice them they go straight into the bloodstream so they can start to help us feel absolutely wonderful. Trace minerals we get from green juicing include:

- ⮑ Calcium – available in foods like broccoli, Swiss chard, mustard greens, turnip greens, bok choy and spinach. Calcium helps to build bones and teeth and prevents Osteoporosis.

- ⮑ Manganese – available in good amounts in lettuces and spinach. Manganese helps to ensure good bone structure, ensures that calcium is absorbed properly, supports the functioning of the thyroid gland, regulates blood sugar levels, metabolizes fats and carbohydrates and makes sure our sex hormones are excreted properly.

- ⮑ Iodine – available in kelp and other sea plants, as well as strawberries, beans, and cruciform vegetables like cauliflower and broccoli, this mineral can help prevent thyroid disease.

- Zinc – this essential mineral is great for the immune system and helps to prevent hair loss in balanced amounts. At also helps to regulate testosterone production. Zinc is in palm hearts and cabbage, lemongrass and sprouts.

- Sulphur – Onions, cabbage and broccoli are great to juice to make sure you are getting enough sulphur. Sulphur is a potent antioxidant and anti-cancer mineral. It can also help prevent the cells from absorbing heavy metals.

- Phosphorous – Phosphorous also helps in bone formation, hormonal balance, energy production, cell repair and nutrient absorption. Phosphorous is one of the most important and predominant minerals in the body. Without enough phosphorous you can suffer from bone decay, tooth decay, and rickets along with a compromised immune system. Fortunately when you juice watermelon, squash, pumpkin, or add ground flax seed to your green juices, you get plenty of phosphorous.

- Iron – Many green leafy vegetables, sprouts and fruits are full of iron. This mineral is responsible for maintaining muscle function, and making sure the blood is healthy. Iron also support brain function and protects against anemia, or iron-poor blood which can cause weakness.

- Copper – Copper is important for all our connective tissues. It keeps our eyes and hair healthy and

- Selenium – Selenium is very important for fighting weakness and fatigue. It can be found in brown rice, but also in trace amounts in vegetables like spinach. An ideal dose of selenium is about w

Important Enzymes in Green Juicing

Green juices are also full of important digestive enzymes, which help to break down food and our bodies to absorb the nutrients from our green juices.

Green Juice Recipes

Here is one of my favorite green juice recipes. Packed with vitamins and trace minerals it is a great juice to start with if you have never green juiced before, because it tastes delicious!

Cucumber Apple Tonic
1 small cucumber or ½ large cucumber
    2 celery stalks
    A handful of parsley
    A handful of spinach
    1 granny smith apple (remove seeds)
    ¼ lime. Mix well after juicing. This recipe provides one 8-ounce serving.

Now that you know about the incredible nutrients in green juices, let's look into alkalizing your body. Read on, chapter three covers this subject in full.

Alkalizing Energy

Alkalizing the Body with Green Juice

Now let's figure out how green juices alkalize the body, which means your pH levels are balanced, and why this is absolutely imperative to staying slim, feeling healthy and looking amazing.

Your body has its own perfect balance between acidity and alkalinity that is usually around 7.5 percent on an acid/alkaline scale of 0 to 14, and the blood can be tested to see its acidity rate. A neutral pH is 7, below 7 is considered acid and above 7.0 is considered alkaline. While this is true overall, each organ has its own perfect alkalinity level.

For example, the stomach has a pH rating of about 1.35-3.5 because it needs to be more acidic to digest food. Blood, must always be alkaline for good health with an ideal alkalinity pH of around 7.35.

Certain foods, like Aspartame (a fake sugar used by the food industry) cause over-acidity in the body. Even if the body is only slightly too acidic – just a 6.5 rating on the acid/alkaline scale, it can be comatose or even dead. Acidic blood cannot absorb nutrients from food and acidity causes cells to stop producing energy. Conversely, juicing with alkalizing vegetables like celery, spinach, barley greens, beets, or mustard greens you can help boost cellular functioning.

Did you know, for example, that many different diseases simply cannot grow in an alkaline body? Colds, flu and mucus become a thing of the past when you green juice to help make the body's blood levels balanced and more alkaline instead of acid.

The easiest way to alkalize the diet is by becoming a vegetarian but if you green juice, that isn't as necessary because you are flooding the body with so many nutrients and vitamins that they often balance out other foods like eggs, meat, and cheese which can cause more acidity in the body. Green juicing can also undo the effects of consuming large amounts of caffeine, drinking alcohol excessively and eating a lot of processed foods that are full of preservatives and chemicals our bodies really don't need.

Alkalizing your diet is also one of the best ways to lose weight. When you green juice, and turn your body from acidic to alkaline, you can count on:

- Lower rates of certain types of cancer, especially colon and stomach cancers
- Clearer skin
- More mental clarity and focus
- Faster weight lose
- More energy
- A better mood

Green juicing is one of the fastest, easiest ways to become more alkaline, overall, so let's get right into creating the perfect green juice. It's as easy as can be!

How to Create the Perfect Green Juice

With all the health benefits of green juicing I know you are as excited as I am about getting right down to building your own green juices from start to finish. This chapter will discuss exactly how to prepare, and consume green juices. It's a really easy process when you know how to do it right.

Here are 8 simple steps to follow:

1. Figure out your goal for green juicing. Are you just starting out? Do you want to lose weight, or boost energy? Are you just trying to get more nutrients in your body or are you going for a full detox program? Are you trying to help naturally cure a specific health issue like acne, or high blood pressure? Knowing these things before you choose your green juice will help you to pick ingredients that are meant just for you, and your own specific needs. Remember that those needs may change over time. That's why this guide is so helpful. You might start out wanting to lose weight with green juicing and then later on, decide you can incorporate some special juices to facilitate an intense workout training program or to help you cram for late night exams. Do you need an afternoon boost to help keep up with your kids? How about a nerve tonic to help you distress? Green juicing does it all, so learning what each ingredient does for you over time can be very beneficial.

2. Make sure you choose a good juicer or blender to do the job. We'll talk more about this is an upcoming chapter, but having the right tools can make your juice habit much easier to stick with.

3. Start with leafy greens. The primary ingredient of almost any green juice is – you guessed it – green! You can choose from spinach, Swiss chard, different lettuces, kale, and more. The leafy greens are all full of numerous vitamins and minerals and can do everything from support weight loss, to boost energy and prevent many forms of diseases from Diabetes to Heart Disease to poor eye-sight, and even depression. Always choose organic leafy greens so that you don't drink a glass full of pesticides and herbicides used in conventional farming. You can visit your local farmer's market or get your greens from a grocery store. You can also grow them yourself. Leafy greens are really easy to grow in containers in a sunny area of your own home, and they can grow all year long. If you have a garden already, congratulations, now you can start juicing your greens!

4. Add a few more alkaline vegetables. This can be as diverse as cabbage, broccoli, cauliflower, carrots, and even sweet potato. You can juice beets, celery, and cu-cumbers; as well as herbs like cilantro, basil, rosemary, or thyme. Almost any vegetable that has high water content can be juiced.

5. Spice it up with ginger or onions for certain green juicing recipes. Both of these juicing options have a very strong taste, but highly medicinal qualities, so you may want to start by adding just a touch to your sweeter juices (like those that contain apples or carrots) and then experiment with adding higher quantities later on.

6. Peel, or cut up vegetables that need to be put through the juicer and then put it all through the juicer to be juiced.

7. Top off with a squeeze of lemon, which will help to keep the juice from oxi-dizing, a fancy word that describes what happens to living matter, like fruits and vegetables, when they are exposed to oxygen. The more a juice oxidizes, the less its nutrients are available for the body to assimilate, so it is best to consume your green juices immediately after they have been juiced. While this isn't always possible, we will discuss ways to store green juices effectively a little later on, plus we'll go over a few juicers that have lower spin rates, so they tend to incorporate less oxygen into the green juice. If you have ever added

lime or lemon to guacamole for a party to keep it from turning brown, you are essentially doing the same thing – keeping the avocados from oxidizing.

8. Serve immediately with a few ice cubes or if you have made a very strong-tasting juice, you can water it down a bit with purified water. If you are serving the juice later, refrigerate it right away.

It's that easy! Green juicing can be fun and variable, and you'll start to feel immediate rewards from doing it, so let's move on to storing green juices for the times you can't juice and drink them right away. We all have busy lives, and sometimes you can't juice when you would want to, so let's figure out exactly how to juice more often by storing our juices properly.

How to Make Green Juice in a Blender

If you just can't get your hands on a juicer, this section will be vital.

If you are using a blender or Vitamix, you will be consuming more of the fiber of the fruits and vegetables that you juice. Don't' expect them to have the same consistency as those green juices made in one of the juicers discussed earlier that extracts the fiber form the fruit or vegetable. You can still get an amazing smoothie from a blender though, and you can even throw in some ice or rice milk, almond milk or wheat grass powder to make your green smoothie extra refreshing and health-boosting.

Don't prepare your fruits or vegetables too soon. Make sure you only cut them up or skin them right before you use them, because this is the food's natural protection against bacteria and oxidation.

You will want to skin all fruits and vegetables, and remove seeds if you are using large-seeded fruits. Things like strawberries are fine to leave as is – just cut the tops of the greens off, if you like, but you can also leave them in-tact and just throw everything in your blender. You may also want to cut the stalks of kale leaves, since they won't blend as well. It is also important to add a little liquid, even if it is just purified water or organic apple cider vinegar to make sure your hard foods blend well.

Make sure you place foods in the blender, lightest to heaviest, since the heavier foods will tend to sink to the bottom anyway. If you are using a blender you can use citrus to help flavor your juice, just be mindful of your 2 to 1 ratio of vegetables over fruits for the healthiest green juice. If you are using a lemon, be sure to peel the skin – the same goes with all other citrus. Also core apples – to remove seeds and stems.

Cut the fruit and vegetables into small enough pieces to tumble around in your blender and be completely liquefied. Add some lemon to keep the juice from oxidizing and enjoy. It's that simple.

Storing Green Juices Properly at Home and on the Go

L et's face it, not everyone has time to make green juices two or three times a day, even if they *really* want to stick to green juicing and make it a lifelong habit. While drinking your green juices right away is the very best way to get all the nutrients and minerals, as well as the 'vital force,' or 'life force' of the fruits and vegetables that you juice, sometimes you will want to store your juices and drink them at a later date.

Here's what you should know before you learn how to store your juice, though:

➲ The beneficial nutrients of your juice will start to diminish in the moments after you juice, no matter what kind of fruit or vegetable you put through your juicer. This includes all the plant-purified water (water from the fruit or vegetable), minerals, vitamins, carbohydrates, lipids, phytonutrients like carotene and lycopene, chlorophyll, etc. This happens because these ingredients are sensitive to air (oxygen), heat, and light. Dr. Max Gerson, famous for the Gerson Institute that helps to naturally treat cancer patients, states that you should consume all fruits and vegetables ideally within 20 minutes of juicing them.

- Some containers will keep your juices fresh longer and maintain their beneficial effects and others are not good for the juice, and can even make them toxic.

- Some fruits and vegetable juices store more easily than others, so if you are going to prepare juice in order to drink your green juices over several days or a week, you will want to use some items and stay away from others.

- There are tricks to keeping your juices fresh no matter if you will drink them later in the same day that you made them, or will drink them at the end of the week.

So how do you store juices in those times you just can't drink them within 20 minutes of preparing them?

- Certain types of juicers prepare juice in a way that makes it spoil less quickly due to the oxygen that gets pumped into the juice as it is made (usually in machines that use centrifugal force are less desirable for storing juices).

- It is preferable to store your juices in glass jars. Mason jars with wide lids so you can clean them more easily, since juices tend to stain are ideal. Plastics are not so great to store juices in because many of them contain toxic chemicals like BPAs that can leach into your juice. Even hard plastics or HDPE plastics (poly carbonate) that are supposed to be o.k. still contain toxins that can seep into your juices and make them bad for you, thus negating their beneficial qualities. You can also store juices in amber-colored jars, since they block out some light, or in stainless steel containers.

- You should always refrigerate your juices if you need to store them. Keeping them cold will keep the nutrients fresh and available for absorption by your body for a longer period. Letting juice stay out at room temperature is one of the fastest ways for it to oxidize.

- Try to fill your juice containers all the way to the top to get rid of the extra air that will oxidize the rest of the contents of your jar, stainless steel bottle, etc. If you don't have enough juice to top off your container, then you can just fill in the remaining space with purified water. Don't use tap water, though, unless you've got your own well and you've had it tested. City water can contain all kinds of toxins, including arsenic!

- If you can use a vacuum pump to take the air out of your juices, this is the most ideal way to store them. Vacuum sealing devices come in both hand-pump and electronic versions; they are often used in canning or jarring jellies, jams or pickles. A mason jar sealer will do the trick quite nicely.

- Always use organic produce. Non-organics tend to be full of pesticides, herbicides, fungicides, and other chemicals that you really don't want to put in your body. GMO (genetically modified foods) are known to cause cancer, organ failure, and even infertility, and over 800 scientists around the globe have demanded a stop to the growing of crops such as soy, corn, etc. that companies like Monsanto and Dow are responsible for planting for these reasons. Why go to the trouble of putting so many good things in your body if you are going to pollute it with non-organic GMO fruits and vegetables? It kind of makes the whole effort a wasted one.

- Pre-chill your containers and use cold vegetables and fruits. Even if you normally enjoy fruit room temperature, make sure that you put both fruits and vegetables in the refrigerator so that when you juice them they don't oxidize as quickly. Also, pre-chilling your containers can help to keep the juice cold.

- Add a squeeze of lemon or lime to all your juices. Citrus is a great way to keep juice from oxidizing, and even though you don't have to juice an entire piece of fruit, just a teaspoon added to your green juices will keep them from turning brown as fast, which means they are oxidizing.

- You can also freeze your green juices right after you make them by placing them in ice cube trays in the freezer. This is a great way to keep them cold, reduce oxidation, keep many of the nutrients in tact, and make a handy way to take your juice to go. If you have a stainless steel bottle, you can through some iced green juice cubes into it with a little purified water and take it with you when you are on the run. Freezing causes juice to degrade faster than when you put it into the refrigerator, so only do this when absolutely necessary. You can also freeze juices in milk jugs or other plastic containers that will take very cold temperatures more easily.

To summarize: drink green juices right away when you can. When you can't, it's important that you keep your juices in air-tight containers and keep them cold. Avoid plastic containers when you can. Overfill, or fill to the brim to keep air out, and use a vacuum sealer if you are able to. When possible use a low rpm juicer or one that does not utilize centrifugal force to extract juice.

Sunflower Sprout Delight

Put all ingredients in a blender and mix well.

> 1 1/2 cups apple cider or juice
>
> 2 cups filtered water
>
> 1 cup fresh pineapple, sliced
>
> 1 cup sunflower seed sprouts
>
> 2 tablespoons hemp or sunflower seeds
>
> 1 tablespoon lemon juice

(Serves 2)

How to Combine Greens, Fruits & Other Ingredients

This chapter will unveil the secrets of combining ingredients for a taste-bud treat and some out-of-this-world health benefits. It will also discuss ratios and amounts.

While there are no hard and fast rules for combining, the 60-40 rule is a good one to start with if you have never green juiced before. This means that you add 40% fruit and 60% vegetables and greens when making your juices – to make sure they taste good and you can get them down the hatch! Let's face it, we could drink something that tasted like dirt if we were told it would cure us form cancer or help us to feel better, but there is no reason to drink green juices that you find distasteful when adding some natural 'sweet' along with the nutrients in many fruits, can really make green juicing not only pleasant, but really enjoyable. You will be much more likely to keep up a habit too, if it is something enjoyable, rather than something you detest and only do because you 'have' to.

If you have been green juicing for a long time, or occasionally you want to really bring out the big guns and eradicate illness or even pep yourself up from a rough or busy week, the you can reduce the fruit ratio in your green juices, but over-doing it can make you feel nauseous, because green juicing is very powerful. The ingredients in a pure green-juice without any fruit at all can be delicious, but many people aren't used to swallowing that much goodness at once.

When, for example, was the last time you ate an entire cucumber, three carrots, two bunches of kale and some lettuce all in one sitting? Not many of us do that kind of eating very often – if you do, great! For the rest of us, using the 60/40 ratio *(60% Fruits and Vegetables 40% Greens)* will make sure that our green juices are nutritionally dense, but also delicious.

If you are doing a juice cleanse, you will drink approximately 80 ounces of juice a day, so it's even more important to make sure that you can drink all the juice you make, by making it extra tasty!

Also, you may hear some nutritionists say that you shouldn't combine raw fruits and vegetables due to the different way that the body deals with their particular set of enzymes, but when you juice just know that fruits travel through our system faster, and of course, contain sugar, and vegetables are usually digested more slowly, so make sure not to overdo the fruit, and you should be just fine.

Additionally, you will never try to juice fruit that has low water content, like bananas or avocados. While you can add these in a blender later to juiced leaf greens, they can't go in your juicer.

Drinking so much nutrition all at once isn't 'natural' per say, even though it is really good for you, so if you drink a juice and it makes you feel nauseous or headachy, you may need to slow down, as you are probably dealing with a healing crisis, which is when the body detoxes too fast and can't get rid of the toxins it is purging from the organs quickly enough.

Also realize that while adding green juices to your daily food intake is wonderful, or doing a periodic green juice cleanse is fantastic, only drinking green juices would eliminate these important things from your diet:

- Essential amino acids/protein
- Enzymes
- Essential fatty acids
- Carbohydrates
- Fiber

This is why green juicing should be combined with healthy meals, or should replace one or two meals a day, not constitute your entire food consumption every day, 365 days a year.

Now, on to some great combinations! The following green juicing ingredients often taste really wonderful together:

Apples–considered a "neutral" fruit and can be combined with vegetables of any kind.

Leafy greens – can be combined with just about anything, but some, like arugula, have a spicier flavor and are better suited to zesty green juices with ginger or a touch of onion.

Kale – this is one of the most nutritionally dense leafy greens on the planet. It has a strong flavor when juiced, but due to its low water content, it doesn't make a lot of juice – just a really powerful elixir once it is juiced. You can blend kale with almost any juice since the small quantity – though full of nutrition – will be very little to overpower as far as flavor, and the other ingredients in the juice will usually round it out.

Celery – since celery has such high water content, it can be used with almost any kind of juice. It also has a very mild flavor and tastes very refreshing, so it goes well with mild-greens and sweet juices, spicy juices like jalapeno and ginger combos and just the regular every-day green juice. It is also a great nerve tonic, so why not add it to just about everything?

Ginger and Carrot – this combination has been used for centuries since the sweet and spicy balance each other perfectly.

Citrus – lemon and lime can be added to almost any green juice that has apples or carrots in it, but may not taste as good with blended juices that use other fruits like bananas, blueberries or strawberries. Lemon and lime can always be added to the aforementioned juices to help keep them from oxidizing – even if they aren't listed in the ingredients of a recipe.

Parsley – this herbal wonder has a bit of a strong taste, so it blends well with a bit of sweet added, like apple, pineapple, or carrot.

Here are a few green juicing recipes to try out different food combinations:

The Hulk

Omega Institute's ultimate green juice recipe! Enjoy!

- 2 Stalks Celery
- 1 Cucumber
- 1 Apple
- 1/2 Lemon
- Ginger
- 1/2 Green Chard Leaf
- Cilantro
- 3-5 Kale Leaves
- 1 Cup Spinach

Sweet Green Juice

This green juice provides super sweet energy! Add kale and parsley first. Then add romaine, cucumber, celery and apple. The apple will sweeten up this green juice for any one who doesn't love the earthy taste of green juices, normally.

> 2 cups Kale
>
> 2 cups Parsley
>
> 3 cups Romaine
>
> 1 Cucumber
>
> 3 Celery Stalks
>
> 1 Apple

Every Day Green Juice

Just juice and enjoy!

> 1 cup Spinach
>
> 2 cups Kale
>
> 2 Cups Parsley
>
> 1 Cucumber
>
> 1 Celery Stalk

Kale Power Green Juice

Just juice and enjoy!

> 3 Carrots
>
> 1 Apple
>
> 3-4 Celery Stalks
>
> 4 Cups of Kale

Ginger Lemon Aide Greenie

Peel or slice the lemon. Leave some of the white pith. It is recommend to roll the cilantro into a ball to compact the leaves.

> 5-6 Kale leaves
>
> 1 Cucumber
>
> 3-4 Celery Stalks
>
> 2 Apples
>
> 2 lemons
>
> 1 Smaller piece of Ginger

Grapefruit Greenie

1 Apple

1 Grapefruit

3-4 Celery Stalks

1 Head of Kale

1 Cucumber

1 Lime

Getting Ready: How to Prepare Ingredients for the Best Green Juices

If you don't prep your vegetables and fruits properly, you can miss out on some of the benefits of green juicing. This chapter covers all you need to know to get it right from the start.

Here are some simple, general steps to make sure you get the most out of the fruits and vegetables that you juice:

- Use organics whenever possible.

- Wash all fruits and vegetables before cutting into them – even ones with skin you won't be consuming.

- Always cut larger fruits or vegetables if you are feeding them into a centrifugal force juicer so that they can be juiced completely.

- Roll leafy greens up into a cylindrical shape before adding to the juicer, and push them through with firmer ingredients to get the most out of them.

- Peel non-organic fruits and vegetables to remove any pesticide remaining.

Use the following list to make preparing a variety of fruits and vegetables easier than ever.

Apples – To prepare apples for juicing, cut them in quarters. While many people don't eat apple seeds, it's fine to leave them in place for juicing. They contain vitamin

B17, potassium, and magnesium, and they're high in protein. If you're using a blender to make your juice, it's best to remove the core and stem to avoid excess wear and tear on the blade.

Apricots – Wash the apricots and either tear them in half or slice them in half to access the pit, which should be removed before juicing.

Asparagus – Asparagus has delicate tops, so use care in washing this vegetable. Push asparagus into your juicer bottom end first.

Avocado – Avocados and juicers just don't mix. If you want to use an avocado in a recipe, juice other ingredients first, then add them to the blender, along with the avocado's flesh.

Bananas – Just like avocados, bananas don't do well in juicers. To thicken a recipe with banana, make your juice first, and then blend it together with the banana in the blender.

Basil – Wash carefully to remove any dirt or sand. Either juice leaves on their own or add stems, too; just roll these up and push them into the juicer with firmer produce.

Beets – Peel your beets under running water, and cut them in quarters before adding them to the juicer.

Bell Peppers – Remove the stems from bell peppers before juicing. Cut them in halves or quarters, and don't worry about removing the seeds. They're a nutritious addition to juice.

Blackberries – Do not wash blackberries until right before using them – washing ahead of time hastens spoilage. Simply rinse in a strainer, and be sure to pick out any thorny stems before juicing.

Blueberries – Like other berries, blueberries shouldn't be washed until just before use. To clean blueberries, simply rinse them in a sieve.

Broccoli – Slice any discolored florets, leaves, or stem parts off broccoli after washing. You can add the whole plant – stems, stalks, and florets – to juices.

Butter Lettuce – Tear leaves from stalk and rinse individually. To add to juices, just roll the leaves together into a cylindrical shape, then push down the juicer's chute.

Cabbage – Either tear off individual leaves or cut sections of cabbage that will easily fit into the juicer's chute.

Cactus Pears – Peel carefully. Cut down to size after peeling if needed.

Cantaloupe – Cut in half, and then scoop out seeds. Cut each half into four sections, and then cut each section into chunks after removing the rind. If you have a melon baller, you can simply scoop chunks from each half of the cantaloupe – put these into a bowl or measuring cup to preserve as much juice as possible.

Carrots – Just wash carrots thoroughly and push them down the juicer's chute. If they're not organic, you'll need to peel them, as well.

Celery Root (Celeriac) – Scrub with a brush to remove any hidden dirt. Peel to prevent an overly earthy flavor if you like; cut this heavy root into quarters to make juicing easier on your machine.

Celery – Remove any really heavy fibers from celery stalks before juicing. After rinsing, simply push through the chute, tops and all.

Chard – Rinse leaves carefully, then roll together and push through the juicer's chute. Chard is often grown in sandy soil, so be sure to use extra care in cleaning this leafy green!

Cherries – After washing, use a cherry pitter or a small paring knife to remove the hard pits before juicing.

Chayotes – After washing, cut down to size, and then push through the juicer's chute.

Cilantro – Cilantro is usually grown in sandy soil and it can retain a lot of sand. Fill a bowl with water, submerge the cilantro, and swish it around to remove the majority of the sand, and then give it a final rinse. Roll up into a ball before adding to your juicer.

Collard Greens – Wash carefully and roll together into a cylindrical shape before pushing into the chute.

Cranberries – Simply rinse and add to juicer.

Cucumbers – If you have a waxed cucumber or one that isn't organic, you'll need to peel it before adding it to the juicer. Otherwise, simply rinse and push down the chute.

Dandelion – Only use dandelion greens harvested from areas where no chemicals are used. Wash the leaves and roll up to add to the juicer.

Dill – Rinse well and add the fronds to your juicer. I like to put them in at the same time as other greens, which I then push through with a cucumber for a nice light drink.

Eggplant – Eggplant is quite bitter and doesn't lend itself well to juicing as it has a firm, spongy texture. This vegetable is one that I don't use for juice.

Fennel – Cut into quarters after rinsing, then put through the juicer. You can juice the tops as well as the bulbs.

Garlic – Try a little at a time and be sure to peel before juicing. Garlic is great with tomatoes, basil, and cucumbers.

Ginger Root – Cut or snap a section off the main ginger root, then scrub it well. Scrape the peel off and add the root to the juicer.

Grapefruit – Peel the zest off with a peeler, retaining as much white pith as possible, since it contains nutrients that help you absorb vitamin C. Cut into quarters or chunks before juicing if it won't fit down the chute whole.

Grapes – Wash grapes, and then remove stems. If grapes contain seeds, don't worry – just add them to the juicer whole.

Jalapeno- Wash, remove top, and cut in half. Remove the pith and seeds before juicing, and be careful not to rub your eyes afterward. A little jalapeno in your juice will help clear a stuffy nose; I find it is also helpful in eliminating headaches.

Jicama – Don't peel jicama before juicing since there are loads of nutrients in and near the skin. Simply slice into large chunks to make the task of juicing easier on your machine.

Kale – Wash carefully, then roll leaves together into a cylindrical shape before shoving down the chute.

Kiwis – Kiwifruit should be peeled before juicing; once you've got the peel off, just drop the whole kiwi into the juicer.

Leeks – Slice in half lengthwise, then rinse between each layer. Leeks are grown in sandy soil, so be sure to clean carefully. The root and green leaves are fine to add to your juice.

Lemons – Peel zest away from pith using vegetable peeler, or if you really love the flavor of lemon and have organic lemons, simply slice in half after rinsing and add to the juicer, peel and all.

Limes – Follow the same procedure as you would for lemons, retaining white pith and seeds. Lime zest can be quite bitter so use caution about adding entire limes to your juice unless this is a flavor you enjoy.

Mangos – Cut away from flat, central seed, then cut into spears or chunks. Mango skin is fine to add to the juicer, but it will contribute a slightly bitter flavor so keep this in mind when preparing this fruit.

Melons – Cut in half and scoop out seeds. Next, either use a melon baller to scoop fruit into a bowl, or cut each half into sections, peel, and drop chunks into a bowl before juicing.

Mint – Wash well, then roll into a ball before juicing. Like other greens, it's best to push mint through the juicer with a firm ingredient like melon or cucumber.

Mustard Greens – Use mustard greens sparingly as they have an intense flavor. Rinse and roll up before adding to juicer with other savory ingredients.

Onions – Remove papery outer skin, and then cut into sections before juicing. The same procedure should be followed for garlic if you choose to use it in savory juice recipes. For green onions, simply rinse well and remove roots, then add to the juicer, green tops and all.

Papaya – Papayas should be cut in half and skinned before being added to your juicer. The seeds are very high in protein and can be added to juices with no adverse side effects.

Parsley – Parsley is normally grown in sandy soil, so it has a tendency to be gritty. Fill a big bowl with water and swish the parsley around to remove sand and dirt, then give it a final rinse. Simply roll it into a ball and add it to your juicer.

Parsnips – These nutty, slightly spicy, slightly sweet root vegetables should be treated like carrots. Just wash the well and add them to your juicer. Peel them first if they're not organic.

Peaches – Cut in half, then remove pit. Add to juicer, fuzzy skin and all.

Pears – Remove stems and cut into halves or quarters before adding to the juicer.

Pineapple – Cut into quarters, and then cut spiny skin away from fruit. Section into spears and add to juice. If the core is woody, remove it; if not, add it to the juicer.

Plums – Slice in half, remove pit, and add to juicer.

Pomegranates – Fill a large bowl with water. Slice the pomegranate in half without pulling the two halves away from one another. Submerge it into the bowl and tear apart, breaking it up into chunks. The seeds will sink and the white pith will float; skim the pith away with a slotted spoon or spatula, then pour the water into a strainer to get to the seeds, which can then be dropped into the juicer. Don't worry if a little white pith remains; it will simply end up in the pulp to be discarded.

Radishes – Like other root vegetables, these can simply be rinsed and added to juice. Skin if not organic, and think twice about using the leaves as they can be very spicy.

Raspberries – As with other berries, wait to wash until just before juicing. Simply rinse in a strainer and be sure to remove any thorny stems or berry caps that might remain.

Romaine Lettuce – Tear individual leaves from the stalk, rinse carefully to remove any sand or dirt, and roll together into a cylinder before adding to juicer.

Scallions – Simply rinse and juice. Add to the juicer root end first.

Spinach–Separate leaves from roots, then wash well to remove any sand. Roll leaves into a ball, and then add to juicer.

Squash – For winter squash, including pumpkins, cut in half, then scoop out seeds. Add these to your juice, as they contain anti-cancer agents. Cut into large chunks after peeling skin. For summer squash, simply cut into large chunks and add to juicer.

Strawberries – Rinse and add to the juicer whole. You can leave the tops on if you like, or cut them off.

Sugar Snap Peas – Simply rinse and run through the juicer, pods and all.

Sweet Potatoes – Scrub thoroughly and cut into large chunks.

Tangerines – As with other citrus fruits, simply remove the zest with a vegetable peeler, leaving the nutritious pith intact. Drop whole into the juicer, or cut in half to fit the chute. If you have organic tangerines and you love the taste of their zest, try leaving all or part of the zest intact to add nutrients and an interesting flavor to your juice.

Tarragon – These tiny leaves are wonderfully flavorful; tear them off their woody stems before adding to the juicer. I like to moisten a firm, juicy fruit or vegetable and roll it around in the tarragon leaves so they stick to it; that way I get as much tarragon flavor as possible into my juice.

Tomatoes – Tomatoes are very easy to work with; just remove the stems, wash well, and add to the juicer whole. If you have very large tomatoes, cut them down to size before pushing them down the chute.

Turnips – Scrub well and cut into chunks before adding to juicer. Although some turnips are small enough to juice whole, they are very hard and can be tough for a juicer to handle and could cause damage if left intact.

Watermelon – Just wash your watermelon, then cut it in half. Use a scoop or spoon to remove the flesh, which you'll want to put into a measuring cup or bowl before adding to juicer. Don't worry about the seeds – they can go right into the juicer without causing any problems, and they'll add a bit of extra protein and minerals to your juice.

Wheatgrass- Rinse and roll into a ball. Now, push it through at the same time with a juicy, firm ingredient like a pear or a cucumber. Most juicers can handle small amounts of wheatgrass when juiced this way, but don't try to add a lot of wheatgrass on its own unless your juicer is designed specifically to extract the juice from it.

Zucchini – Scrub zucchinis well before juicing, and simply cut the tough stem end off. A zucchini makes a great mild-tasting addition to any green juice!

Selecting a Juicer:
Top Tips for Juicing Success

You won't want to continue juicing if you have a lousy juicer. In this chapter I'll cover three possibilities in a low, medium, and higher price range, so that you can get the best equipment to juice right!

To begin let's look at 8 things you may want to consider before purchasing a juicer:

1. Too much fruit juice is not a good thing, since it is full of sugar. Even natural sugar in excessive amounts can cause health problems, so you need a juicer that can handle fiber-filled fruits and meaty vegetables. A juicer that is typically used to juice oranges, or other citrus, for example won't work for green juicing. You need to make sure that you are juicing vegetables, and lots of green ones. Drinking green juices helps to ensure that you don't consume too much fructose, the primary sugar in fruit. When consumed excessively, this can lead to a glucose problem called insulin resistance; it can also create more triglycerides which can lead to heart health problems.

2. You will still need to eat your vegetables. Drinking green juices is important, and can greatly affect your health in a positive way, but you can us the fiber in vegetables too. The fiber can also make you feel fuller and produce a feeling of satiation so that you don't want to eat excessively, so consider purchasing a

juicer that allows you to keep the pulp and use it for composting or even putting fiber into baked goods like zucchini muffins or banana bread.

3. Make sure that you are modifying your overall calorie intake based on the nutrients you are consuming since green juices are packed with nutrients. You may want to reduce calories somewhat, and do so safely, without neglecting your overall health to make sure you aren't getting too many calories. After all drinking your food puts some calories down the hatch quite efficiently.

4. Most juicers will take large quantities of vegetables and fruits and turn them into very small, compact, nutritionally dense doses of liquid. This means you will need to be committed to purchasing fresh, ideally organic produce on the regular. It would be purposeless to purchase a good juicer and then never use it because you weren't committed to buying (or growing) your produce to use with it.

5. Juicers are not inexpensive, in most cases, and if you plan on staying with this healthy habit, you will want to invest in a decent juicer that won't break down after a few uses, or leave you with a stalled or burnt-out motor. If you aren't ready to make the investment in a juicer, perhaps start with just eating more organic greens and upgrading your healthy lifestyle in other ways until you can afford a good juicer and are committed to using it consistently. Even juicing for two people can require an industrial strength juicer, and if you are juicing for a whole family or group, you will definitely want to invest in a high quality juicer that can handle the volume of juicing you are planning to do. You can get a good juicer for just over $100 – spending any less than that might be foolhardy. Be sure the juicer you choose comes with a warranty.

6. Larger juicers take up space, are harder to clean and will need to be stored when out of use. This is also an important consideration when purchasing a juicer.

7. Expect to commit some time to juicing. Just like cooking a great, healthy meal, juicing can take a few extra minutes to do – by the time you purchase your produce, clean it, prep it, and feed it through the juicer, then clean it. It is very much worth the effort, but unless you have a housecleaning staff and gourmet chef at your service, it does require a time commitment.

8. In most cases a juicer with less than 1000-watts of power will be a total waste of time and money. The more wattage, usually, the better the motor will run and therefore, the better centrifugal force juicers will work. Of course this does not apply for juicers that apply pressure as their primary means of juicing.

So how do you choose the best juicer for your personal juicing needs? Let's start with the types of juicers that are out there for you to purchase.

There are five main types or juicers or juice extractors, each with their own benefits and disadvantages:

1. Centrifugal Juicers – these are by far the most popular and most often purchased juicers on the market. They are found in department stores and big box stores like Costco, Sam's Clubs, Shopping Clubs, Target, etc. They are often upright and round in shape to accommodate a sieve that spins at high speeds via a motor, which helps to extract the juice from the pulp or flesh of the fruit or vegetable. They essentially grate the produce into tiny pieces in order to extract the juice. The Jack Lalanne is a popular centrifugal juicer that advertises a large mouth for feeding fruits and vegetables into your juicer with greater ease, but there are many others made by multiple manufacturers with many different price points – ranging from $50 to $1000 ore more.

   Some of the advantages of a centrifugal juicer are that they are both fast and convenient. Often the larger juicers have a large mouth or feeder so you don't have to cut up your fruits and vegetables into smaller pieces, which reduces prep time when making your juices. They can be easier to clean that some of the other juicers out there, but the sieve can get clogged easily and requires a special cleaning brush to make sure all the small bits of fruit and vegetable fiber is removed completely before the next use.
   Disadvantages of a centrifugal juicer include the fact that they don't always juice leafy greens very well, and this is one of the best things about a 'green' juice. They also can make a lot of foam form the spinning action which oxides the juice faster.

2. Masticating Juicers are also known as single gear juicers – these use a screw-type auger to grind, or 'chew' fruit and vegetables, essentially crushing them until their juicy goodness pours forth. These types of juicers also send the juice and pulp into two different containers so you can utilize them both.

   The advantages to a masticating juicer are that it does a better job at extracting juice from leafy greens and fruits with pulp. This means you get more nutrients out of your produce. They also last a lot longer, since there isn't a motor that will burn out as easily as with centrifugal force juicers, so often they have warranties that last 10 years or more, and are therefore sometimes worth a larger investment. These types of juicers can also make more than just green juices. They can make nut butters, sauces, baby food, and even pasta or fruit sorbets.

The downside of the masticating juicers is that they often have smaller mouths so you have to prep your produce more meticulously – cutting things into smaller pieces before you can feed them into the juicer. They are also more expensive, usually, although the higher-end centrifugal force juicers are in the same price range as medium range masticators. Popular brands for the masticating juicer are the Omega 8005/8006 and Champion brand, but there are literally hundreds out there to look at and compare.

3. Triturating Juicers are high-end juicers meant for serious green juicers only. Many people consider these the Ferraris of juicers available on the market. They work much like a masticating juicer, only the motor runs slowly, so the absolute maximum of nutrients and juice can be extracted form the produce – whether it is a piece of kale or a very watery stalk of celery. These juicers also have two interlocking screws that 'chew' the fruits and vegetables very diligently to extract the juice. These juicers result in the driest pulp (which means the juice is packed with nutrients), and therefore you get the most nutrients for your money, invested in both the juicer itself and in the produce that you are juicing.

    Like the masticating juicers, triturating juicers can also make nut butters and baby foods, etc. but they are also costly. They are not as convenient to use and it requires some manual force to push denser foods like carrots into the gears while they are twisting. The Green Star Brand is a popular triturating juicer.

4. Wheatgrass juicers – these are juicers dedicated to juicing grasses like wheat or barley. They cannot juice other fruits and vegetables. Centrifugal juicers won't work on large amounts of grasses – in fact if you shove a large bunch of grass into a centrifugal juicer, it will simply be chewed up. You'll run the risk of burning the motor out in the process. You also wont' really get any of the juice and thus the nutrients, out of the grass if you try to put large amounts through a centrifugal juicer at one time. However, a wheatgrass juicer is designed specifically for this purpose. Note – you can do small amounts of grasses in other juicers. Roll the grasses into a tight little ball and push them through with a firm, juicy item such as a cucumber. Don't try to do more than a very small handful at once.

5. Citrus juicers – like wheatgrass juicers, citrus juicers can only juice one kind of fruit – citrus, which can also be juiced in centrifugal, masticating or triturating juicers, so in many cases you might as well get a one of the aforementioned kinds of juicers unless you will specifically be juicing a whole lot of oranges, lemons, limes, grapefruits, etc.

Choosing Well-Manufactured Juicers

Three are many brands of juicers to choose from but quality of manufacturing can make juicing something you fall in love with, or something you dread. Some juicers are over-priced for what they offer, and some are just plain junk, thrown together without any care for their long-term use. Always choose a juicer, not matter which of the six types listed above, from a well-known manufacturer that offers a warranty on its manufac-tured goods. In the case of more expensive juicers, it may even be worth purchasing the additional warranty that some of them offer for full coverage of parts and service just to protect your investment. An extra $70–$100 for a name-brand with a good warranty can translate to an entire decade of juicing without hassle.

3 Juicers for Comparison in Multiple Price Ranges

Under $100 – The Breville BJE200XL Compact Juice Fountain 700 Watt Juicer is a good low-end juicer. This is the lowest wattage juicer I would recommend purchasing, and only if you are juicing for two individuals or fewer. It is just under $100, but has gotten good reviews on multiple sites. It has a 3-inch feeder tube, which is pretty large, and therefore convenient if you want to reduce prep time for your fruit and vegetables. It takes up less space (only 9 ½ wide by 16 inches tall) than some pricier juicers and comes with a one-year manufacturer's warranty. In general, this is a good juicer for the low price it is offered at.

$300 Masticating Juicer – a good midrange juicer is the Omega J8005 Single-Gear Commercial Grade Masticating Juicer. It functions as a juicer, food processor, homogenizer, baby food maker, and pasta extruder. It processes juices at only 80rpm so they are more nutrient filled and less oxidized as with higher rpm juicers like centrifugal force driven machines. Due to this process, juices can be stored for up to 72 hours before they start to lose their nutritional value.

$1500 Triturating Juicer – A quality triturating juicer like the Super Angel Juicer 5500 is going to cost you a pretty penny, but it retrieves the most juice, and therefore the most nutrients from the organic produce you invest in. It is made entirely of stainless steel, based on 25 years of manufacturing innovation to come up with its design. It can juice wheatgrass as well as an apple or carrot, so it takes the place of multiple juicers with more singular capabilities. It juices fruits, vegetables and grasses at a very low 85 rpm so the enzymes and nutrients stay intact and are not exposed to excessive oxygen which reduce their nutrient quality. It utilizes twin gears to 'eat' the food you are juicing for incredible results.

Taking Care of Your Juicer

If you invest in a great juicer, no matter its price-level, you want it to last, and keep it clean so that you don't contaminate the items you juice. This chapter gives you tips and tricks about how to make your juicer last as long as possible.

Prior to Juicing Your First Green Juice

You should always take your juicer out of the box, and though you will be excited to use it right away, make sure you take the few extra moments to read the manufacturer's instructions before you try to operate your green juicing machine. Read and re-read these instructions because they will be full of important things you need to know specific to your juicer. For instance, "motor will not run when the locking bar is not in place." Or "do not try to remove the sieve while motor is running or the juicer will not work." Some times these things seem like common sense, but especially with juicers you've invested your hard-earned money in, and that come with a bigger price tag, you will want to be sure that you don't ruin your investment before you've even had the delight of drinking your first green juice!

The manufacturer's instructions will also usually give some good tips about how to keep your device clean, which is essential to making nutrition-filled green juicers regularly.

Washing Your Juicer

After every single use of your green juicing machine not matter the type, you will want to clean it. You are putting organic matter through this machine. It rots. It spoils. It can spread disease and bacteria if not washed properly, so it is vital to do this every time you use it. It will also prolong the life of the machine if you keep it clean. Where blades are involved, it keeps them rust proof, and where sieves are involved, a clean juicer, keeps from spreading bacteria through non-pasteurized juices, which is what you are making.

Storing The Juicer

When the juicer is not in regular use, it should be stored in a safe place where it won't be exposed to dust and debris. If you plan on keeping the juicer on your countertop, either make a cover, purchase one, or cover it with the cover that the manufacturer provides, if there is one. Also always unplug it from the wall outlet to protect it from power surges, and also because it will lower your electricity bill since your juicer won't be pulling a micro-charge called a phantom charge by being plugged into an outlet all the time.

Getting Started With Green Juicing: Easing Your Way In

I know you haven't been chugging the green stuff since you were just out of your mother's womb, but hopefully you will make this a life-long habit by starting slow and sticking to it. I'll tell you how.

The best way to start green juicing is a little at a time. There are many seasoned green juicers who only juice greens, for instance, they will make a kale-broccoli-cucumber-celery juice and drink with a look of delight on their faces. Kale is a very strong tasting green when juiced, and so are greens like broccoli, collar greens, bok choy, etc. Experienced green juicers have grown to love the taste of these foods blended with various things with a less strong taste like cucumbers or celery.

For others, the taste of green juice is not something they are used to, so they need to acquire the taste over time. Usually people really appreciate how green juicing makes them feel, so whereas, in the beginning they will want to add more sweetness to their juices with things like apples and carrots, later on they are willing to experiment with having a lower fruit content in their juices, until they don't juice fruit at all. This is probably the healthiest way to green juice, since once fruit is separated from its fiber, its like pure sugar being poured into your bloodstream. Juicing fruits without greens to balance them is far from ideal.

In the best circumstances you would eat fruit with its accompanying fiber so that the fructose would be absorbed more slowly into your body, and you would also get all the great antioxidants and enzymes in the fruits. It isn't as if fruit is the enemy.

The thing is, that vegetable juices – particularly green vegetables – is one of the healthiest things your body can consume and when you prepare your juices with a larger proportion of them being green vegetables, you will feel even more amazing than when you drink vegetable-fruit combinations.

Also, the body is usually addicted to sugar and processed foods – almost like a drug, so it can take some time to wean your taste buds from wanting things that are overly sweet. After you cleanse your palate some, you will notice that refined sugars and processed foods just don't taste 'good' anymore. You will also be so grateful for the new-found energy and clear-headedness that you feel when you green juice, that you will be more likely to seek it out as a way to get your calories, instead of by less healthy alternatives.

Since taste and sugar content are important factors to consider when you first start to green juice, you will perhaps start with one green juice (mixed with no more than 1 part fruit) every day. You will also want to go slow for reasons besides taste and sugar content, however. This is because, while high nutritional levels are wonderful for your body, you can trigger a healing 'crisis' if you dump too much good stuff into your body too fast. Drinking green juice is so powerful that it can trigger toxin-release from your organs – your kidneys, liver, digestive tract and even your skin. If you start to get headaches or feel nausea or greater fatigue in the first weeks that you green juice, this is usually a sign that your body is detoxing. Don't give up! If the symptoms of the detox process are too intense for you, you can always lessen the amount of green juices you consume, and steadily but slowly increase them as your body has a chance to get used to new levels of health and fitness.

Following are a few great green juicing recipes for beginners; these are not only tasty, but full of nutrition!

Green Juice for Beginners
Juice all ingredients and enjoy. Serves one.
  2 medium apples
  1 celery stalk
  1 leaf of lettuce or kale

Ginger Pear Delight

Juice all ingredients and enjoy. Serves one.

- 2 medium Anjou Pears (or any variety to substitute)
- 1 stalk of celery
- 1 thumb-sized piece of ginger (adds a spicy flavor to the juice)

Summer Watermelon Cooler

Juice all ingredients and enjoy. Serves one.

- 2 cups diced watermelon
- 2 leaves of Romaine lettuce
- 1 celery stalk
- 1 medium carrot

Keeping It Up:
Enjoy a Daily Juicing Habit

Once you start green juicing, don't stop. I will show you how to keep the healthy habit of green juicing going, even when life is hectic and spending the extra time to green juice seems like a chore. If you follow these simple steps, you will be able to continue this health-giving habit and not back-slide into eating more unhealthy foods and processed junk in place of the juices that make you feel incredible and fuel your body through the busiest days.

- Keep your recipes simple. The less you have to think about it, the better, especially when you get really busy. If you have a long weekend and you can dream up elaborate juices and new recipes, go for it, but in the mean time, use a few great ingredients and keep it simple.

- Put a sticky note or a 'love' letter to yourself on the refrigerator that says, "I deserve to feel great and I'm tired of being sick, fat, and tired." Every time you see this it will create a new neural pathway to promote the new healthy habit of green juicing that you are trying to create. It can take up to 90 days to change behaviors that no longer serve you, so if you want green juicing to stick, make sure you drink at least one green juice daily for 90 days to help 'lock it in' as a new, healthy habit.

- Start with juicing several times a week and only slowly integrate a few juice fasts (where you only drink green juices for a day or so) to really cleanse the body of unwanted toxins and renew health and vitality. Don't go too fast, too quickly or you won't stick to it.

- Pair your new healthy habits. One reinforces the other. Once you start green juicing you will feel better. It is likely you will want to be more active or take on the world from a new, more energized level. Try adding a new gym habit or invite a friend to go on evening walks with you as you green juice. Doing more thing one good thing for yourself at a time helps to reinforce the healthy lifestyle you are creating.

- Have fun with it. Invite friends to try new recipes with you. Experiment with different green juices with family members. Make your green juices fun, and you will be more likely to keep it up.

- Juice first thing in the morning. If you juice first thing, when your belly is empty, you will absorb all those nutrients and start off your day feeling great. All the other disruptions and demands of the day won't matter, because you've already done one good thing for your self before you've even set foot out of the door. This also means that if you happen to have time to juice again later in the day – great, but you've gotten at least one green juice in right at the start, so you're good to go!

- Take your green juices to go. If you can't green juice first thing in the morning. Prepare your juices the night before and store them in a container that you can quickly grab from the refrigerator and take with you.

How to Prepare
a Weekly Shopping List

Now that you know about all kinds of greens and the benefits they can provide you, let's learn exactly what you need to do to keep a green juicing habit going. It all starts in our weekly trip to the grocery store, or if you're lucky enough, in your own organic garden. Since we don't all get to grow our own organic vegetables, you can start with a simple list to take with you depending on your needs.

Since you know that all green juices start with a green, add another alkalizing vegetable, and then a small portion of fruit with some lemon juice, you can combine different flavors to make a great juice and then ass those ingredients to your shopping list. Some recipes will be simpler, others more complex, so obviously this will change your grocery list. The more you can vary your ingredients form week to week, the better, that way you can get all sorts of vitamins and nutrients from the different fruits and vegetables – the rainbow of health that is offered by Mother Nature! You will want to shop for your greens one week at a time, maximum, and if you happen to live really close to a store that you can visit more often, try to shop more frequently to keep your juices as fresh as possible.

A sample grocery list for just one kind of green juice consumed daily for one week follows:

- ⮑ 6 granny smith apples (x 7 days) = 42 granny smith apples (you can often be these in bulk)
- ⮑ 1 ½ bunches of kale (x 7 days) = 11 bunches of kale
- ⮑ 3 organic lemons
- ⮑ 1 organic lime
- ⮑ 7 cucumbers (x 7 days) = 49 cucumbers
- ⮑ Small ginger root
- ⮑ 7 baby bok choy
- ⮑ 21 medium sized organic carrots with greens attached
- ⮑ 2 gallons of purified water (reverse osmosis or distilled)

This grocery list would make one 8-ounce glass daily of the following recipe:

Green Zinger
1 organic granny smith apple
1 ½ bunch of kale
1 squeeze of lemon juice
1 squeeze of lime juice
1 organic cucumber
1 baby bok choy
3 organic carrots
1 ½ inch size piece of fresh ginger root

Mix all ingredients in juicer except for lemon and lime juice. Add a touch of purified water (to taste) and squeeze lemon and lime at the end. Enjoy this zesty, tangy, nutrient packed green juice zinger.

The best way to figure out how to shop for your green juices is to figure out which juices you will be making in one week, and then calculate the total ingredients needed for each juice. Buying organics in bulk is a great way to save money when juicing since many items juice down a relatively small amount of juice (like kale) while others provide abundant juice, depending on water content (like celery or cucumbers). Don't let the amount of juice that a particular food item creates fool you though; even a teaspoon of kale juice down the hatch is like pure nutritional gold to your body and worth way more than if you ate five meals of junk food found at a drive through or fast food restaurant. If you just calculated what you would spend on unhealthy food, and then compared it to the life-saving benefits of green juicing, you won't mind spending just a few extra dollars a week to heave more energy, lose weight, and feel absolutely amazing.

Some people buy their produce 3 days at a time due to space constraints. This is fine, too. You will want to modify your shopping list so that you will be sure to use all the items before they spoil. It would be better to under-buy and then make an extra trip, than to throw out great, fresh, organic produce that you don't use.

One of the simplest green juicing recipes for seven days would have a shopping list as follows:

- ➲ 18 bunches of Kale

- ➲ 5 heads of Arugula (approximately 70 leaves)

- ➲ 30 medium organic carrots

- ➲ 3 organic lemons

Straight Green Energizer

   2 ½ bunches of kale
   10 leaves of arugula
   3 med. organic carrots
   1 squeeze of lemon
This recipe makes one 6-ounce glass of pure, green juice.

Blend all items in a juicer and squeeze lemon after the juice is poured into your cup. Enjoy.

If you were doing a straight green cleanse, where you only consumed green juice and water for seven days, you would just multiply the above shopping list by 4. This would provide you with 4 juices a day. You normally increase the amount of juice you consume when you are doing a juice fast so that you don't get as hungry, and it flushes your body with insane amounts of nutrients.

Overall, the amount of produce you need to buy depends on the type of green juicing you are doing. Your overall goals might be to overcome a health problem, lose weight, cleanse the liver or kidneys, and increase energy level or a combination of things.

Trying to figure out what fruits and vegetables to buy once you are at the grocery store instead of calculating it out before you go will often lead to waste – not just of the food – but of money, so be sure to do a rough calculation before you go shopping and always bring your list!

Going All the Way: The Importance of Organic Produce

One of the first things you need to be sure you do when you green juice is use organic fruits and vegetables. They can be slightly more expensive, but juicing with traditional or GMO, meaning genetically modified crops, is one of the most important things you need to do when you decide to green juice.

Organic produce is grown without pesticides or chemicals in the fertilizers that are used, as well as without using genetically modified seed which has been known to cause everything from cancer to organ failure, and even serious reproductive health issues if eaten consistently over a long period of time.

Not only is your health better, but you are helping to protect the planet when you eat organic vegetables and fruits instead of those laden with toxic pesticides, herbicides, fertilizers and other unnatural ingredients that were never meant to be in the human body. Many fertilizers are made from fossil fuels, and they deplete the natural richness of good, organic, composted soil. Some studies coming out are even saying that soil depletion due to modern agricultural practices is so extreme that many of the fruit and vegetables grown now are much less nutritious than the same things grown even 40 or 50 years ago.

While you won't get sick from eating trace amounts of pesticides or industrial fertilizers on your food, when you juice *everything* is intensified. This means the good, the bad and the ugly. You don't want to pour gallons of nutrition filled fruits and vegetables down the hatch – loaded with enzymes, phytonutrients, vitamins, and vital minerals, just to top it off with a heaping glass-full of toxic chemicals. You may as well drink poison!

That being said, organic foods, especially if you have a family and you are considering juicing for more than just yourself, can be expensive, so below is the Environmental Working group's annual list of the dirty dozen foods – that is the foods analyzed utilizing data from the Department of Agriculture about pesticide use and the residue that is most likely still on your fruits and vegetables when you buy particular variety that you purchase. This group has done the work for you so that you don't have to guess about which produce to purchase.

They estimate that you can reduce pesticide exposure by up to 80% just by avoiding the following 'dirty dozen' foods that are usually the worst when it comes to toxic pesticide remains:

1. Apples – this fruit is delicious but they are often prone to pests and therefore are sprayed quite liberally with pesticides so that farmers don't have to worry about fungus and insects eating their crops. Apples are also often treated with antibiotics, so it is smart to go organic when you want to add apple juice to your green juices.

2. Celery – the USDA has found more than 60 different pesticides in use on celery. If you are going to juice this great nervous system-boosting vegetable with high water content and tons of antioxidants, it is best if it's organic.

3. Cherry Tomatoes – They may look like cure little bundles of love on the vine but they are often sprayed with toxic chemicals. Only buy your cherry tomatoes from a local, organic grocer, if possible.

4. Cucumbers – while you can peel their skin to reduce the possibility of pesticide exposure, cucumbers are still laced with pesticides in numerous forms, so skip the chemical toxins and buy organic instead.

5. Grapes and Raisins – this great fruit is often laced with toxic chemicals, so buy organic form your local farmer's market or health food store.

6. Hot peppers – though these hot peppers a common ingredient in green juices, they are still a great way to boost your metabolism and clean the blood. An occasional green juice with peppers it quite delicious and health-boosting. Hot peppers unfortunately make the dirty dozen list, though, so get your jalapenos and hot peppers organically whenever possible.

7. Nectarines – most nectarines are imported and they are full of pesticides. Buy this delicious fruit organic.

8. Peaches – this is another tree fruit that is often sprayed. Avoid conventional peaches and go for organic.

9. Regular Russet Potatoes – though rarely juiced, sweet potatoes have become a popular green juicing root vegetable to add to certain recipes. Avoid the pesticide ridden Russet potatoes and other varieties sold at your supermarket and buy organic instead.

10. Strawberries – although these are often blended instead of juiced, strawberries are full of pesticides if you don't buy organic.

11. Spinach – this is an important leafy green vegetable in many green juicing recipes, but it needs to be organic. Try buying in bulk to save money.

12. Sweet bell peppers – these peppers have a high pesticide residue according to the FDA. Try to buy them without the extra toxins.

There are lots of fruits and vegetables that are still sprayed or treated with herbicides and fungicides that are not on this list, so if you can simply buy everything organic, all the better. I try to stick with some bulk-purchased staple organic leafy greens and then buy whatever organic produce is on sale and incorporate those items into my green juices to keep my healthy habit on the affordable side of the shopping equation. No one wants to go broke trying to be healthy. So, as stated in the previous chapter, just keep it simple and if exotic fruits or vegetables catch your eye, purchase organic wherever possible.

Now, if you really want to keep an eye on your budget, you can also purchase the following 'clean 15' foods that are not necessarily full of toxic residues and pesticides.

These are safe to purchase as non-organics:

1. Onions. These vegetables are left alone by many insects, so they don't have to be sprayed as often. Buy them as a conventional food product.

2. Avocados. Due to their thick skin, which isn't consumed, it is safe to purchase avocados without buying organic.

3. Sweet corn. This crop doesn't take a lot of fertilizer to grow and it is covered in a husk, but do look out for GMO corn which is one of the biggest crops produced by Big Pharma companies like Dow and Monsanto.

4. Pineapple. Again because of its thick skin, pineapple is rather immune to pests, and therefore o.k. to purchase as non-organic.

5. Mango – although you should rinse them well even before removing the skin mangos are relatively safe as a non-organic food.

6. Asparagus – this is also a relatively safe item to purchase non-organically. Just try to buy asparagus that is bright green with purple, compact tips, to make sure they are fresh and full of vitamins and nutrients.

7. Sweet peas. According to the Environmental Working Group, sweet peas are safe to purchase non-organically.

8. Kiwi. This fruit has a furry barrier in the form of their skin to protect them from pesticides.

9. Cabbage. For some reason, cabbage doesn't attract lots of pests, so it doesn't have to be grown with lots of chemicals. This vegetable is safer to purchase non-organic than many other vegetables.

10. Eggplant. This brightly colored, purple vegetable is another safe vegetable to put on your non-organic shopping list.

11. Papaya. This fruit should always be washed thoroughly before consuming but grows well without lots of pesticides.

12. Watermelon. Due to its thick skin, watermelon should be washed and then eaten. The pink flesh is protected from chemicals used in farming.

13. Broccoli. This crop doesn't retain pesticides as many vegetables do. So, it is better to purchase this non-organic than other things like spinach.

14. Tomatoes. Not to be confused with cherry tomatoes, regular beef-steak and other varieties of tomatoes can be companion planted with other plants so that they don't require as many pesticides to grow.

15. Sweet Potatoes. While regular potatoes are grown with lots of chemicals, sweet potatoes seem to get by unscathed. Purchase your sweet potatoes as a conventional food instead of organic if you need to.

Green Juicing on a Budget

Many people mistakenly think that green juicing is too expensive to develop a habit for it. This is simply not true. I'll show you how to stay green juicing on the cheap.

First – look at the dirty dozen and clean fifteen. Make sure you take these into account when you go chopping for juices. No matter what green juices you feel inclined to make, think about varying recipes depending on what is on sale. I also look on eBay for coupons for organic produce, visit farmers markets, sing up for food co-ops with friends to get loads of organic fruits and vegetables that we share, and even volunteer once a week at a community garden so that I can take home a bundle of organic veggies and fruits to green juice – plus I'm helping my community eat healthier. You don't have to sacrifice your health or your budget in order to green juice. There are numerous ways to get good organic produce on a budget.

Consider these ideas to lower your food bill:

- Volunteer at a community garden that grows organic fruits and vegetables. There are usually numerous community gardens in every city and they can always use help. The best part is that you will get to take home some of what you grow and also learn how to organic garden for yourself should you ever decide to.

- Buy in bulk at big box stores. If you can get 5 pounds of organic spinach to juice all week instead of the small bags they sell at the regular grocery store why would you pay more? Also, forget shopping at the over-inflated health food stores for the bulk of your green juicing items. You can get carrots, celery, and greens for much cheaper, and organically, if you purchase them in bulk. Just get the items like organic lemons or limes, for example at your health food store- they will often double the price as compared to a big box store.

- Buy your produce on sale. If celery is 2-for one this week, then incorporate it into more of your green juices. This seems like a no-brainer, but many people have simply forgotten how to look for sale items when they shop for their green juicing ingredients.

- Save money on health care bills when you green juice. Even though it is a bit of an investment in your health up front, many people need to visit their doctors less often, so they incur reduced medical costs.

- Use coupons. Many organic items can be purchased at a discount with coupons. Check the Whole Foods circular, or sign up at MamboSprouts.com for organic coupons to take with you when you green juice shop.

- Use a rewards card at your grocery store. It may take an extra few minutes to sign up for one, but sometimes stores will offer deep discounts to their 'preferred customers.'

- Use 'buy one get one free' offers often used by food retailers to promote specific items in their stores.

- The website LocalHarvest.com will tell you where to buy organic produce locally. Sometimes purchasing organic produce from local farms can cut out the middleman and reduce your costs of purchasing enough greens to juice consistently.

- Amazon has a 'subscribe and save program' which can save you up to 15 percent on food products.

- Buy in season. Fruits and vegetables that are grown in accordance with their natural growing season are always less expensive.

- Start growing your own organic vegetable. There are tons of DIY lessons on how to start your own organic garden, no matter if you have several acres you can plant on, or just a small window box on a terrace in a large city. Growing your own organic food to use in green juices and delicious recipes is not only healthy but very gratifying.

Green Juicing: An Amazing Way to Detoxify the Body

In this section we will get down to the nitty-gritty about why it is so important to cleanse the body's organs and detoxify with green juicing.

None of us feel good when we are stopped up with toxic chemicals. There are literally thousands of environmental toxins that we consume via our food, through the air we breathe and the water we consume. Green juicing helps to remove many of those thousands of toxins so that we can be the healthiest version of ourselves.

How to Detox With Green Juices

From here, we'll go straight into the basic facts about why you will want to detox the body with green juices and exactly how the liver, blood, and other important detoxifying organs of the body need some help —green monster juices to the rescue!

Once the body is detoxed form green juicing, it does everything better, and more efficiently—from metabolizing food to giving you lot's of great energy to have fun and play throughout your day.

This section will include many different recipes specifically designed to help your body detox from ten of the most common environmental poisons like:

- ⮑ Pesticides: Almost all of the pesticides, herbicides and fungicides used by the non-organic farming industry are known cancer-causing toxins. These toxins also cause impaired fetal development, nerve damage, and even fertility issues. You can remove almost 99% of these with green juice; as long as it's organic. This happens rapidly when you eliminate certain foods that contribute to your toxin load, because the body has a chance to cleanse itself. Thanks to the nutrients green juices contain, which go rapidly into your cells upon ingestion, your body gets the opportunity to actually focus on releasing toxins.

- ⮑ PCBs: (polychlorinated biphenyls) PCBS are used mostly in the building of transistors, electric motors and capacitors. They were banned from the US for several decades, but persist as organic pollutants in many countries. The most prominent way people consume PCBs now is through farm-raised salmon. Salmon are fed smaller fish, which are contaminated with the toxin. PCBs cause cancer among other undesirable diseases. They also block your body's ability to absorb nutrients from the foods you eat. Green leafy vegetables that are juiced and sent straight to the blood are great for detoxing PCBs.

- ⮑ Mycotoxins: (mold and fungal toxins) these toxins are in contaminated buildings, foods like peanuts, corn and some alcoholic beverages. They cause asthma, multiple sclerosis, diabetes, heart disease and cancer. Just a small amount of mycotoxins can cause trouble in your body but green juices flush them out every time.

- ⮑ VOCs: (Volatile Organic Compounds) These toxins also cause ozone depletion and air pollution. Sometimes they are even worse in the air of our homes and offices than the air outside. They can be found in drinking water, air fresheners, many cosmetics and body scrubs, washes, and soaps, paints, deodorants, cleaning fluids and the chemicals used in dry cleaning. VOCs have been linked to cancer, respiratory problems, headaches, dizziness, and memory problems. Consuming plenty of filtered water and green juices is an excellent way to rapidly flush these toxic chemicals from the body.

- ⮑ Phthalates: These chemicals are in plastic wrap and almost all plastic food containers, and are used to soften plastics or prolong their life. Your endocrine glands cannot produce the right kinds or levels of hormones when you consume too many phthalates because their structure chemically imitates that of many hormones already naturally present in the body. Certain green juices help to detox phthalates and other endocrine disruptors very well. For example, those made with broccoli sprouts help to stimulate the body's production of the enzymes which eliminate toxic estrogens like those found in foods packaged in cans lined in plastic coating containing BPA (bisphenol-A), which is a toxic xenoestrogen.

- Dioxins: These toxins come from burning things like wood coal or oil. In the process of incineration, dioxins are releases into the air, water and soil. These toxins can cause cancer, a severe acne problem, reproductive disorders and interfere with fetal development. You can reduce dioxins from your diet by eating less animal fats, but green juicing helps get rid of dioxins too!

- Heavy Metals: These toxins are many and include aluminum, mercury, lead, arsenic and cadmium. They can collect in our body's tissues and cause all kinds of problems from Alzheimer's disease to cancer, fatigue, nausea, vomiting, impaired thinking, an abnormal heartbeat, and damaged blood vessels. Just one great green juice addictive, cilantro, is great for detoxing heavy metals, but there are many more.

- Asbestos: This industrial toxin was used in buildings widely from around 1950 to 1975. It was used as insulation on floors, ceilings, and around water pipes and ducts but when it gets old and crumbly, it breaks off into dusty pieces that contaminate everything around it – air, water and soil included. It can scar lung tissue, and cause a rare form of cancer called mesothelioma, but green juicing cleanses it right out.

- Chloroform and Chlorine: This toxin comes from chlorinated water. It can cause cancer, birth defects, liver and kidney damage, sore throat, wheezing, lung collapse, dizziness and fatigue. It is found in drinking water and household cleaners, but you guessed it, green juices can help eliminate this toxin from the body.

With all these toxins (and this is just a brief list) I know you will want to green juice as fast as possible to start getting them *out* of your body!

Detox With Green Juice: Cleaning the Guck Out of the Liver and Blood to Lose Weight and Feel Great

Maybe you've already tried a bunch of different 'diets' that promised you that you could lose weight according to whatever fad of the moment is most in vogue. That's just plain silly. You probably figured out that even when you lose weight utilizing many of these 'latest craze' diets that you gain it right back and often with a few extra pounds to boot. The problem with many fad diets is that they don't address one of the most important issues about weight loss, and that's detoxing the body.

Green juicing is so incredible at helping to clean the toxins out of the liver and blood, its downright uncanny. Who knew that detoxing could be so easy? Green juicing using natural, organic foods can heal the body and it starts by cleaning out the liver. Let's look at why this is so important.

The Liver is one of the Most Important Detoxifying Organs

The liver is so important for detoxing the body, that if it can't do its job correctly, we become fat, sick, and tired. If the liver completely stops working, then we can even die.

The liver is the body's filter. It might be called the hardest working organ in the body, and that says a lot considering it only weighs about five pounds. It sits next to the heart and works even as you sleep.

The liver detoxes the body in three ways:

1. Through bile production

2. Through the blood

3. By changing toxins into water soluble materials that can be excreted from the body, essentially neutralizing toxins

The liver makes bile and bile contains acids that are very important for digestion and absorption of nutrients, but also of fats and fat-soluble vitamins that hang out in the small intestine. Waste products like bilirubin are eliminated form the body via feces through the bile acids.

As adults, we will produce about 400 to 800 milliliters of bile every day. It happens in two stages. First the hepatocytes (part of the main tissue of the liver) will secrete bile into microscopic canals of the liver. Hepatic bile contains bile acids, cholesterol and other organic goodies that your body needs to digest foods and food waste. Next, the bile flows through the bile ducts and turns kind of watery so that the epithelial cells can utilize the bile.

Certain foods promote liver detoxification; as you've probably guessed by now, detoxifying your liver is one of the best things you can do for your overall health.

- Garlic and onions are great for adding to spicy green juices. They contain a sulphur-based compound allicin, which helps to eliminate mercury, harmful food additives, and toxic estrogens.

- Cruciferous vegetables including Brussels sprouts, broccoli, cabbage, and cauliflower are ideal for adding to nearly any juice recipe. These vegetables contain chemicals that neutralize toxins including nitrosamines, which are found in cigarette smoke, and aflotoxin, which is a toxic compound found in peanuts. These vegetables also contain powerful glucosinolates, which help the liver to produce the enzymes it requires for healthy detoxification.

Why Green Juicing and the Liver Are Best Friends

To put it simply, without bile, made by the liver, the body could neither take in nutrients or get rid of stuff your body doesn't need. Even more importantly, *without proper bile production, and bile acids, you can't lose weight*! You shouldn't even consider trying to lose weight if your liver is clogged and toxically overloaded!

Green juicing helps to detox the liver in very specific ways:

- The liver's main job is to aid the lipase enzymes to digest fats; if your liver or gallbladder (where bile acids are stored) are not working properly, fats and toxins will not be broken down correctly and will start building up, thereby causing weight gain. Artichoke increases bile production , and helps the liver to function properly so that these toxins will be eliminated rather than building up. Studies show that bile production can increase by as much as 100% after the nutrition from a single globe artichoke has been consumed.

- The liver is the largest internal detox organ, so it should be your best friend when it comes to weight loss. When you eat poorly, the liver actually makes more fat (to store the toxins in) and keeps you overweight. Green juicing is one of the best ways to detox the liver so it will stop making excess fats. Adding apples to your green juices introduces pectin to your body's system. Pectin helps to bind toxins so that they are eliminated rapidly, thus helping weight loss continue at a healthy rate.

- When the liver is 'feeling better' it starts to work more efficiently and you free up energy to move more. You will have boundless energy after green juicing and actually want to be more active and exercise. Add fruits and vegetables that are high in antioxidants to your juices to help protect the liver from the free radicals that are produced during detoxification. Dark colored berries, pink grapefruit, plums, and purple grapes are excellent choices.

When we make the liver work overtime by eating lots of refined sugars, unhealthy fats, food preservatives, GMO foods, non-organic foods, homogenized milk, fertilizers, pesticides, hormones that are fed to animals that in turn are killed for meat products, nitrates, heavy metals, etc. then the poor organ gets exhausted. Green juicing gives the liver what it needs to do the work of off-loading all the incredible poisons we put into our body every day, every week, every month – for years! Can you imagine? If you worked that hard you might need a vacation too!

Even more fascinating is that when you mask the symptoms of an overloaded liver (and essentially a toxic body) with painkillers or antibiotics (because trust me, a toxic body *will* get sick more often) the immune system becomes depleted and you can possibly develop long-term, chronic illness and yes, **more weight gain**.

It's worth noting that fat cells hold a ton of toxins, it is kind of our bodies' way of keeping us 'safe' and still able to get up and do what we need to do every day. As we get rid of the fat, we also get rid of the toxins, and vice versa. A less toxic body is a thinner body, but also a healthier one.

Getting Rid of an 'Estrogen" Belly

Another way that green juicing helps to detox the liver is by eliminating 'estrogen dominance,' caused by xenoestrogens (unhealthy estrogen hormones that come from GMO crops like soy, primarily) that build up in the cells and cause the body to develop more estrogen which makes for a higher rate of fat storage. Estrogen is often thought of as the women's hormone, but we all have estrogen in our bodies as part of a healthy and natural combination with other sex hormones like progesterone and testosterone. Menopausal women can have an especially hard time with weight loss, since the body naturally starts making less of the other hormones like progesterone and testosterone as well as human growth hormone to help balance out the estrogen.

When these hormones become out of balance at any age and in both men and women, it can make us age faster and hold onto fat, often causing many diseases. The 'pot belly' that many people have, again, observable in both men and women, is often due to an estrogen imbalance. Men may call it their 'beer gut' or even develop 'man boobs' due to this problem of too much estrogen. The liver is one of the primary organs responsible for getting rid of xenoestrogens so that we don't develop these unsightly problems.

Remember, adding green juice to your diet is only part of the health equation. To fully cleanse your liver and keep it clean, and to prevent future problems with toxic weight gain in the future, do your best to eliminate foods that cause this. Now that you know more about how the components in green foods help promote detoxification, and now that you know how certain components in common foods promote toxicity, don't you feel inclined to transform the way you nourish your body?

The following recipes are delicious; more importantly, they are designed to help promote healthy detoxification and speed up the healing process so that you can lose weight while gaining energy and providing yourself with a whole new outlook on life. Try to have at least one of these green juices each day; two to three is the ideal number. However, if you are detoxing too rapidly and experiencing uncomfortable side effects, cut back and allow detox to happen at a slower pace.

Green Liver Live-It-Up Recipe:

This great green juice recipe calls for Parsley, Dandelion and Green Tea Extract, all wonderful liver cleansers:

> 3 bunches of organic parsley
>
> 2 tsp. green tea extract (powder or tincture form)
>
> 1 large stalk of celery
>
> 1 small organic apple
>
> 1 tsp dandelion herb or one ½ cup of dandelion tea

Juice the parsley, celery, and apple, then stir in the green tea extract and dandelion herb or tea. You can use a blender to get a better consistency if desired.

Grapefruit Liver Cleanse

This juice contains a pinch of cumin powder, which together with the fruits, garlic, and parsley help to detoxify the liver while supplying it with vital nutrients.

> ¼ Cup purified water
>
> 2 Lemons, peeled
>
> 2 Grapefruits, peeled
>
> 1 Bunch organic parsley
>
> 1 Inch section ginger root, peeled
>
> 1 Garlic clove, peeled
>
> A pinch of cumin powder

Juice the lemons, grapefruits, ginger root, parsley, and garlic. Mix these juices with the water and then mix in the cumin powder. Drink immediately.

Veggie Detox Blend

Light and slightly sweet without being overpowering, this blend contains cabbage, celery, and pear, all of which aid in rapid detoxification.

> ¼ Cup purified water
>
> 5 Ounces green cabbage, chopped
>
> 1 Lemon, peeled
>
> 1 Stick celery, thick strings removed
>
> 1 Pear, roughly chopped, stem removed

Juice the cabbage, lemon, pear, and celery. Blend the juice with the purified water and drink immediately.

Healing Beet Detox

Beets help to purify the blood and relieve the heavy load the liver carries. This juice has a slightly earthy flavor and a beautiful dark green color that tells you it's going to go straight to work within your body.

    ¼ Cup purified water
    1 Medium beet, peeled and cut into quarters
    1 Large carrot
    1 Cup baby kale or spinach

Juice the beet, carrot, and baby kale. Stir together with the purified water and drink immediately.

Cucumber Beet Detox

With a light flavor and plenty of minerals, this detoxifying juice helps to purify the blood and nourish the liver as well as the rest of the body.

    1 Cucumber
    1 Stick of celery, thick strings removed
    ½ Beet, peeled and cut into quarters
    1 Large carrot

Juice all the vegetables and drink immediately. As the cucumber is mostly water, there's no need to add any extra water to this recipe.

Cabbage Cleanse

Raw cabbage juice helps to eliminate toxins, while celery, pears, and watercress are also powerful cleansers. Add more pear to the blend if it tastes overly bitter.

    ½ Small cabbage, chopped
    2 Pears, stems removed
    2 Sticks celery, thick strings removed
    2 Handfuls watercress

Juice all ingredients and drink immediately. If the mixture is too thick, add a little purified water.

Lemon Wheatgrass Juice

This simple juice neutralizes toxins and helps the liver to heal itself. Be sure to use a wheatgrass juice extractor or chop your wheatgrass and process it in the blender to avoid damaging your juicer.

    4 Ounces wheatgrass
    1/2 Lemon, peeled
    1 Cup purified water

Juice the lemon, and if you've got a wheatgrass juicer, juice the wheatgrass. If you have no wheatgrass juicer, mince the wheatgrass and add it together with the water and lemon juice in the blender, processing just until smooth. If you're using juicers, just mix the juices together with the water. Drink immediately.

Super Green Detox Juice

The high concentration of chlorophyll this juice contains helps the liver to expel toxins while aiding in healing.

>   2 Sticks celery, thick strings removed
>   2 Handfuls baby spinach
>   1 Handful parsley
>   1 Handful kale
>   1 Handful lettuce
>   1 cucumber

Juice all greens and vegetables. As the cucumber contains plenty of water, there's no need to add extra. Drink immediately.

Fruity Liver Cleanse

If you're new to juicing and are still developing your palate, you'll appreciate the mild taste this fruity liver cleanse offers.

>   1 Handful kale
>   ½ Beet, peeled
>   10 Green grapes
>   2 Green apples
>   ¼ Lemon
>   ½ Grapefruit

Juice all fruits and vegetables together. As the lemon and grapefruit contain plenty of liquid, there's no need to add purified water unless you find the juice's flavor to be overpowering.

Apple Carrot Liver Cleanse

Dandelion leaves aid the liver in expelling toxins, while the pectin in the apples helps to carry those toxins away.

>   ¼ Cup purified water
>   2 Large carrots
>   1 Green apple
>   ½ Lemon, peeled
>   1 Small Handful dandelion leaves

Juice carrots, apple, lemon, and dandelion leaves, then stir in water. Drink immediately.

Super Citrus Detox Blend

Just as some commercially prepared medications can be a little hard to swallow, this blend has a pungent taste. Don't let the flavor stop you from healing your liver – this potent blend helps eliminate toxins rapidly so your body can work toward better health.

> 4 Lemons, peeled
> 2 Grapefruits, peeled
> 2 Cloves garlic
> 2 Inches ginger root
> A dash of cayenne pepper

Juice the lemons, grapefruits, garlic, and ginger root together. Next, sprinkle the cayenne pepper on top and mix it in thoroughly. Drink immediately, then consume a glass of purified water with a slice of lemon in it.

Green Juicing:
Great for Weight Loss

You will next learn how to lose weight with green juicing, kill sugar cravings for good, and supplement solid food in the event you want to replace an entire meal with a green juice. This, just by itself, is a highly motivating reason to start enjoying more green juices.

The Glycemic index of the foods you eat can be confusing, but by green juicing you automatically reduce sugar cravings that can cause your glucose levels to take a nose dive and cause crazy food cravings that in turn lead to binges, which over time, cause you to become obese.. Can you imagine not even wanting to eat cookies, cakes and donuts anymore? What could be more amazing than that?

You see, drinking undiluted green juice is like eating pounds and pounds of nutrition. Most of us are overfed but undernourished, so reducing our caloric intake while providing our bodies with the nourishment they need eliminates both problems at the same time.

The truth is, we overeat and snack on junk foods because we are starving for *real* food. We feel hungry because the body is literally dying for the vitamins, minerals, phytonutrients, micronutrients and macronutrients it needs to stay healthy. The reason we reach for potato chips or chocolate cake or any other unhealthy snack when we feel tired, stressed, or run-down is because we need *real* food. By consuming these types of filler foods, which contain simple sugars and man-made fats that cause us to crave more crappy foods, we only make the original problem worse. When we fill ourselves up with the power-packed nutrition in green juices, we change our body chemistry and start *wanting* to eat different things.

Replacing unhealthy foods helps in another way, too. When we consume plenty of green juices, our energy levels are restored so going out and being active is something we actually *want* to do. We won't want to sit around on the sofa watching television all day – we will have too much energy for that and our bodies will send us signals demanding that we get up and move. With green juicing, getting exercise becomes a joy instead of a chore, because you have a surplus of energy that needs to be used up.

So, green juicing leads to a thinner waistline, and it's also a way to de-stress without causing damage to the body. After all, exercise is one of the fastest ways to release endorphins– and these powerful brain chemicals pave the way for a better mood. Do you see how all of these things are starting to relate to one another? When they come together, they work to create a better version of you – the real you, the one you've always longed to become.

Many people ask why green juicing works better than simply eating all the fruits and vegetables you use in your juice. While there's no problem with eating plenty of fruits and vegetables each day, there's just about no way you could work your way through a huge pile of produce day after day. Would you be able to sit down and eat a whole bundle of kale leaves, two big green apples, a whole cucumber, and a lemon all at once? Most of us wouldn't be able to do that, so if you said "no" to that question you certainly are not alone.

Juicing promotes weight loss by giving the body what it needs. It extracts nutrients and it allows for easy access to the many important enzymes fruits and vegetables contain.

Here's how it works, in a nutshell:

- ⮑ Insoluble fiber is removed from fruits and vegetables that go into your juicer.

- ⮑ Removing that fiber makes it easier for your body to absorb the nutrients it so desperately craves.

- ⮑ The healthy phytonutrients, enzymes, and soluble fiber (necessary for heart health) remains in the juice.

- ⮑ Fresh juice is consumed immediately to prevent these healthy components from oxidizing.

- ⮑ Nutrition is immediately delivered to the body, which starts using those nutrients right away to cleanse itself of toxins and feed cells that are struggling to stay alive.

Once the body reaches the appropriate level of nourishment for maintenance, it goes into overdrive, healing damaged tissues, promoting healthier hair and skin, and completely reprogramming itself. As this occurs, cravings for unhealthy foods are eliminated.

It's important that I mention here the importance of continuing your new, healthy green juice habit even after you've lost the weight you initially set out to eliminate. Green juice feeds your body on a cellular level, but those cells need that good nutrition to keep pouring in. Without it, cravings will return and you'll rapidly find yourself back where you started.

Besides drinking green juices while losing weight and afterward, it's vital that you make good food choices:

- Keep eating lots of fruits and vegetables.

- Try not to consume processed foods, particularly those that contain gluten, added sugar, or chemicals of any kind. Be very choosy about what you put into your body.

- Limit your consumption of animal products if you choose to eat them at all.

- If you do have animal products, stick to low-fat versions without a lot of chemical additives. Choose organic, humanely raised meats, dairy, and eggs to ensure you're getting as little toxic intake as possible. If you're anything like me, you'll find your taste changes and you may no longer want to consume these items. If that's the case, fantastic! You'll feel better and you may even live longer.

- Try new raw foods. Super foods like chia seeds, flax, and spirulina can be added to anything without changing the food's flavor.

- Drink plenty of purified water and avoid water from plastic bottles that contain BPA. Mild dehydration feels a lot like hunger, and staying hydrated will help you lose weight and keep it off.

Finally, don't overlook the importance of exercise. We need to move to stay healthy, and to keep our lymph systems clear. Pick activities you enjoy and spend a little time each day moving your body.

Here are a few low-calorie green juices you can start juicing to kick-start a weight loss program:

Low Cal Grapefruit Greenie

1 Grapefruit
Peeled & Cored Pineapple
2 Cucumbers
Bunch of Spinach
Large bunch of Kale
Bunch of Parsley
Truvia or other stevia sweetener to taste

Peel grapefruit, cucumber, pineapple and juice. Enjoy!

Summer Splendor

This tasty juice is only very lightly sweet, plus it fills you up.

1 Small cucumber
2 Stalks celery with long fibers removed
1 Large carrot
1 Ripe tomato
½ Peach, pit removed
½ Orange, peeled
1 Handful baby spinach

Juice all ingredients. Pour into a glass and enjoy!

Sweet and Spicy Greenie

This juice looks fantastic in the glass and tastes just as good. The jalapeno is an unexpected ingredient that amps up flavor while giving metabolism a boost.

½ Fresh Pineapple, cut into chunks
2 Stalks celery with long fibers removed
1 Handful kale
1 Handful spinach
1 Handful parsley or cilantro
¼ Jalapeno, seeds removed

Juice all ingredients. Pour into a glass and enjoy!

Citrus Surprise

This delicious juice contains plenty of greens – the surprise is that it's actually a red color in the glass! If you find this recipe too tart, add a little stevia to balance the flavor.

> 2 Medium beets, peeled and cut into quarters
> 1 Large handful kale (about 6 large leaves)
> 2 Medium oranges, peeled (use blood oranges if available)
> 1 Ruby red grapefruit

Juice all ingredients. Pour into a glass and enjoy!

Hearty Pumpkin Spice Delight

If you're feeling puckish, try this hearty juice. It has a sweet, mellow taste and plenty of soluble fiber so it fills you up and keeps you feeling full. Cinnamon helps to tame hunger pangs and reduce cravings, so use as much as you'd like to.

> 1 Inch ginger root
> 1 Pear, stem removed
> 2 Large carrots
> 2 Tart apples
> 2 cups Pumpkin, chopped with seeds removed
> 1 Cup butter letuce
> Cinnamon for sprinkling

Juice all ingredients except cinnamon. Pour into a glass, top with cinnamon, and enjoy!

Plum Perfection

Though this juice contains lots of greens, it also contains plenty of deep blue and purple fruits that give it an appealing purple color.

> 2 Ripe plums, pits removed
> 1 Pint fresh blueberries
> 1 Inch ginger root (optional)
> 1 Large handful red leaf lettuce

Juice all ingredients. Pour into a glass and enjoy!

Green Berry Zinger

This juice may look a little funny at first; but pour it into a glass and allow it to separate for a few moments, and the green will float to the top while the red berry juice will rest on the bottom of the glass. Suddenly, it looks like a festive yet low-calorie treat!

8 Strawberries

6 Kale leaves

2 Celery stalks, long fibers removed

1 Sweet apple (golden delicious is a nice choice)

Juice all ingredients. Pour into a glass, allow to rest for a few moments, then enjoy!

Green Kiwi Cooler

This beautiful juice is green in every sense of the word – even the fruits it contains are green!

3 Kiwi fruits, peeled

1 Medium cucumber

2 Celery stalks, long fibers removed

1 Green or yellow apple (Granny Smith is perfect for this recipe)

½ Lemon, peeled

1 Handful greens, your choice

Ice

Chill all ingredients, then juice. Pour over ice and enjoy!

Luscious Apple Greenie

This light-tasting juice is perfect for breakfast. You'll be amazed at how rapidly it delivers an energy boost to your system.

1 Zucchini, stalk removed

1 Green apple, such as a Granny Smith

1 Medium cucumber

3 Celery sticks, long fibers removed

6 Leaves Bibb lettuce

Juice all ingredients. Pour into a glass and enjoy!

Green Melon Cooler

Melons are light and delicious, and are ideal for creating weight-loss juices. This one is wonderful on its own or over ice.

2 Cups Honeydew Melon, cut into chunks with seeds removed

2 Celery stalks, long fibers removed

1 cucumber

½ lemon, peeled

Juice all ingredients. Pour into a glass and enjoy!

Pear Perfection

Pears contain lots of soluble fiber to help promote heart health while keeping you satisfied, and they lend this recipe a delicious, mild taste you'll appreciate.

3 Ripe pears, stems removed

3 Celery stalks, long fibers removed

1 Handful Italian parsley

6 Romaine lettuce leaves

Juice all ingredients. Pour into a glass and enjoy!

Green Juicing: A Great Way to Fight the Negative Effects of Stress

In this section you will learn just how damaging stress is and exactly what green juicing does to reduce its horrific effects on your body, mind, and over all well-being.

Stress is a killer. It does everything from make us fat to wreck our immune systems to make us irritable and angry. It can even trigger clinical depression if not taken care of when it starts to take over our lives completely.

Green juicing is a very effective way of changing how our bodies deal with stress. Let's face it – we all have extraordinary demands on our time and energy, as well as our emotions in the world today – this is unavoidable. You can use green juicing to keep your hormones balanced and your energy levels high, as well as balance out your blood sugar levels so that you don't add more stress to your life by being sick and unhealthy.

You might wonder how simply drinking green juices could possibly help you to eliminate much of the stress you feel in your life. While it is absolutely true that the fact you have made the decision to drink green juices won't stop your boss from handing you extra assignments, won't stop your kids making messes, and won't make other drivers wake up and follow the rules of the road, these juices do change how your body reacts to stressors – and that's what really counts.

When the body is not receiving proper nutrition, stress takes an even greater toll on health. When you juice regularly and consume healthy foods, you nourish your body from the inside out. This leads not just to better physical health, but to less stress, too.

- Consume calories regularly. Your brain needs glucose to perform, and without it, feelings of stress can become overwhelming. Green juices that contain fruit deliver glucose to your system, where your brain has ready access to the nutrition it needs.

- Vitamins and minerals are necessary for stress reduction. The fruits and vegetables fresh juices contain have high levels of vitamins A, C, and E, as well as plenty of zinc, copper, manganese, and other essential minerals. These important nutrients neutralize the harmful molecules your body produces when it's under stress, so you feel less of its negative effects.

- Enjoy plenty of fiber. The modern diet is woefully lacking in nutrition, and it does not offer enough fiber. The healthy fiber found in vegetables, fruits, legumes, and whole grains helps you feel satisfied, helps your body function well on every level, and increases your alertness level while reducing stress – mostly because the action of digestion keeps blood circulating and keeps toxins moving out of the system as they are produced. Remember that juices have plenty of soluble fiber, so even if you're replacing some meals with juice in order to lose weight, you will enjoy these benefits.

- Slow down caffeine consumption. Relying on caffeine to stay awake or alert, or to "improve" performance in any area of your life is a mistake. Caffeine increases blood pressure and contributes to stress. It makes anxiety seem more intense, and it is addictive. Instead of counting on caffeine to wake you up in the morning and keep you moving throughout the day, focus on getting plenty of quality sleep. You'll find you consume less caffeine and you'll notice that your stress level decreases as a result.

As you can see, proper nutrition is holistic in nature. It's not just about calories in, calories out; instead, it's about ensuring that every cell in your body – including the important cells in your brain – get the exact nutrients they need to perform properly. Feeding your body the right way, with plenty of green juices, ensures everything works properly.

After just a short time, you'll notice that consuming lots of green juices on a regular basis leads to an overall improvement in body function – and in brain function, too. Feed your body right and it will work properly. Don't, and you'll be miserable, stressed, and overweight.

In addition to green juicing you can try some of these clinically proven ways to de-stress and feel happier every day:

- Practice yoga, tai chi, qi gong, or meditation. All of these practices have been cultivated for thousands of years with a direct effect of lowering our stress and helping us to feel healthier, happier and more centered. In recent studies, just 20 minutes of yoga a day was proven to add to our mental clarity and significantly lower anxiety levels, and meditation practiced for just ten minutes a day can drastically reduce our feelings of depression, unworthiness, frustration guilt, overwhelm, etc. – essentially all the things that make us feel stressed.

- Walk in nature – nature has a significant effect on us when we feel stressed. The primary colors in nature, blue and green, have a physiological effect on our nervous system to help calm us down. It also helps to expand a limited perspective if we look out over a large body of water or gaze up into an infinity blue sky. Try to spend at least an hour a day outside to help yourself feel less stressed.

- Spend time with friends – the positive psychology movement has proven that spending time with friends can be more effective at lessening stress than even visiting a shrink.

- Watch a funny movie – laughter cures. Laugh as often as you can. It helps to boost the immune system, helps you to stop ruminating about your own problems and boosts mood.

- Eat healthfully and exercise. The more you move the better you will feel since your body releases natural endorphins when you exercise. The more you eat nutrition-filled foods, the more likely you will want to move. This brings us to green juicing. It works. It's easy and it helps you to distress in a big way.

De-stressing with Green Juices

Green juices have an amazing way to change your hormonal levels and boost happy hormones so that you feel incredible when you green juice. Green juicing is like nature's Prozac, only without side-effects!

For example, just one glass of green juice can help to create more serotonin and melatonin as well as the cuddle-hormone, oxytocin, and other feel-good hormones that make stress-causing hormones like cortisol and adrenaline start to decline.

Here is a breakdown of the hormones that green juicing help to balance and why they are important:

- ⟳ Increase of Serotonin – Neurotransmitter responsible for making us feel good, happy and satiated after eating

- ⟳ Increase of Melatonin – Neurotransmitter responsible for feeling that everything is ok with the world even under stressful circumstances. It also regulates the sleep cycles.

- ⟳ Increase of Oxytocin – the love or cuddle hormone which allows us to feel close to someone and experience greater intimacy

- ⟳ Reduction of Estrogen Dominance which causes obesity and irritability

- ⟳ Reduction of Cortisol–Causes the parasympathetic nervous system and brain to feel stressed.

De-stressing and boosting your energy levels with green juicing can literally change your life. And it's a well-known fact that elevated stress can lead to weight gain, particularly around your middle. The question is, why does stress lead to an overabundance of belly fat?

The most harmful fat is found deep inside your belly, and it is often associated with stress. When you're feeling stressed, the hypothalamus and pituitary glands start a conversation with the adrenal glands, which are located on top of your kidneys. These secrete chemicals that increase heart rate, which is why when you're feeling overly stressed, you might notice that your pulse rate increases.

There's another thing that happens during this conversation between your body's glands too. The adrenal glands secrete steroids that instruct deep belly fat on an organ called the greater omentum to increase. In a healthy body, this organ is flat and thin, and a little greater than the size of one of your hands held flat with fingers outstretched. When stress strikes and becomes overwhelming, and when the omentum is instructed to grow, it can become very large and pendulous, weighing in at several pounds instead of just a few ounces.

If the stress continues, the steroids your body releases continue to tell the omentum to grow. So finding ways to address stress including the ones we talked about before is vital to stopping that harmful belly fat and shrinking it. If you're stressed and overweight, you will never become fully healthy until you eliminate the stress from your life. It's best to take a multi-prong approach to stopping the stress that's making you fat and unhappy, and what better place is there to start than with green juices?

Simply improving nutrition will help eliminate stress, but some particular fruits and vegetables contain specific nutrients that help your body to produce important feel-good chemicals and turn those negative messages off so your belly gets smaller rather than larger. In general, all fruits and vegetables contain high levels of the nutrients your body needs to stave off stress; here are just a few of the very best:

- Spinach – Spinach is high in tryptophan, which is an amino acid that elevates mood and promotes relaxation. It is also high in magnesium, which we'll look at more closely in just a moment.

- Beets – Beets are full of minerals that aid in relaxation. If you can't find fresh beets, carrots are another good choice.

- Broccoli – Broccoli contains high levels of the B vitamins that are necessary for healthy serotonin production.

- Celery – Celery contains plenty of vitamins as well as a high level of potassium, which is an essential nutrient in combating high stress levels.

- Citrus Fruits – Lemons, limes, grapefruits, oranges, and other members of the citrus family contain plenty of vitamin C, which helps to strengthen the immune system, which becomes depleted when the body is working to stave off stress. Tomatoes and red peppers are also great sources of Vitamin C.

- Green Leafy Vegetables – Green leafy vegetables contain high levels of magnesium, which helps you to relax and sleep soundly, and which also helps nerves send signals to one another. This nutrient helps to maintain a healthy nervous system too. The mainstay of green juices is leafy greens, so each time you consume one of these delicious concoctions, you'll be helping your body to fight off stress.

Without the right nutrients, you'll be more irritable, depressed, and anxious; you'll be likely to remain tense whenever you're feeling pressured, and you'll sleep poorly. You might even suffer from muscle spasms associated with tension. Luckily, the green juices that follow, along with many others in this book, will help you to fight stress from the inside out.

Stress-Less Green Juice
    1 Large Carrot
    3 or 4 Stalks Broccoli
    3 Stalks celery, long fibers removed
    2 Large handfuls spinach

Juice all ingredients. Pour into a glass and enjoy immediately!

Mood Boosting Mandarin Juice

    4 Mandarins or clementines, peeled

    1 Ruby red grapefruit, peeled

    1 Large Carrot

    2 Celery stalks, long fibers removed

    1 Handful spinach

Juice all ingredients. Pour into a glass and enjoy immediately!

Pineapple Pick-Me Up

    1 Cup fresh pineapple, cut into chunks

    1 Pear or apple, your choice

    1 Head romaine lettuce

Juice all ingredients. Pour into a glass and enjoy immediately!

Ginger Ale Greenie

    2 Celery stalks, long fibers removed

    3 Tart green apples (Granny Smiths are very nice)

    1 Large cucumber

    1 Lime, peeled

    2 Inch piece of ginger root

Juice all ingredients. Pour into a glass over ice, and enjoy!

Green Lemonade, Tropical Style

    ¼ Fresh pineapple, cut into chunks

    1 Small cucumber, or half a large one

    1 Green or yellow apple (try a Golden Delicious)

    ½ Lemon, peeled

    1 Handful Spinach

Juice all ingredients. Pour into a glass and enjoy! Great as is or over ice.

Chill-out Lemon Cooler

    8 Cups spinach

    ½ Cucumber

    2 Granny Smith Apples

    1 Pear

    2 Lemons, peeled

Juice all ingredients. Pour into a glass and enjoy! Lovely over ice.

Bright Green Stress Relief

3 Celery stalks, long fibers removed

3 Leaves kale

4 Carrots

2 Sweet Apples, such as Fuji or Golden Delicious

Juice all ingredients. Pour into a glass and enjoy!

Bloody Mary Juice

4 Ripe Tomatoes

2 Red peppers

1 Hot pepper, seeds removed

1 Carrot

1 Zucchini

1 Large handful fresh cilantro

Juice all ingredients. Enjoy over ice, minus the alcohol associated with this cocktail.

Good Morning Mood Booster

2 Oranges, peeled

2 Apples, your choice

2 Red grapefruits, peeled

2 Celery stalks, long fibers removed

2 Handfuls greens, your choice

Juice all ingredients. Enjoy over ice, minus the alcohol associated with this cocktail.

Ginger-Pear Perfection

2 Apples, your choice

2 Ripe pears

1 Inch Ginger root

1 Handful greens, your choice

Juice all ingredients. Enjoy as is, or pour over ice for a tasty and relaxing treat.

Green Juicing: The Fastest Way to Get Amazing Energy

Here you will learn how to boost your energy pre-and post-workout, or just to get through a demanding day. You don't need to count on caffeine or energy drinks, which are really bad for you. Green juice to the rescue!

One of the best ways to increase your energy naturally is through consuming large amounts of the green goodness which makes green juices their bright emerald or neon-green color. Chlorophyll! We've talked about chlorophyll in previous chapters, but it really is the secret to high energy without consuming a bunch of caffeine that can inhibit your body's natural sleep patterns, and cause insomnia. If you are worried about having enough energy for your day, and you are used to drinking coffee, tea, or even an energy drink, in order to get the vitality you need to handle your responsibilities, then just *try* green juicing. It won't let you down.

Also make sure that you juice with mostly greens, and very few high-sugar fruits so that you don't spike insulin levels in your blood. While this will give you a temporary boost in energy, it will be followed by a nose-dive, as your insulin levels crash right after being elevated. It is always after a 'sugar-high' that we experience a 'sugar-low' so be sure that you don't send your body into a roller coaster ride by drinking high-fructose juices, and never drink juices made in the grocery store or pre-bottled. These are pure sugar and no good for you! Nothing can replace the pure energy of green juices.

Many of the ingredients listed in your super encyclopedia of green juicing foods shows the items that are high in B vitamins. This is another natural way to boost your energy. In fact, many 'energy' drinks that contain caffeine and high levels of sugar also contain high levels of B vitamins in order to give your sustained energy. Why not skip the ingredients, like sugar and caffeine, which are really unnecessary for boosting your energy levels, and green juice instead? It is much more healthy for you and you won't experience a crash or the addictive pull of caffeine from drinking an energy drink with a fancy name in a flashy can made to trick you into thinking you are doing something good for yourself.

If you decide to eliminate caffeine from your life, there are a few things you should know. First, quitting caffeine, like quitting any addictive substance, can be difficult. If you're still on the fence about giving up coffee and other sources of caffeine, you should be aware of the many problems it can contribute to when used in excess.

These problems include:

- Increased risk of high blood pressure
- Keeps the liver occupied so it has difficulty eliminating other toxins
- Contributes to tooth decay
- Can contribute to weakened bones
- Increases feelings of anxiety
- Can cause hyperactivity and difficulty focusing, followed by a "crash"
- Disrupts natural sleep cycle
- Has been linked to hypoglycemia and may interfere with weight loss
- Contributes to dehydration, which can be mistaken for hunger and which can ultimately lead to weight gain and increased toxicity

Consider the items on this list, and think about whether continuing excessive caffeine intake is really worth the potential risks associated. If you'd like to quit, create a large list with these items on it, and put it somewhere you can see it frequently. Seeing this list will help you stay motivated.

Once you've made the commitment to quit, recognize that it is possible for you to overcome your caffeine addiction. Also, when you see positive books about caffeine, you need to recognize that most of the research has been paid for by companies that produce caffeinated products. They want you to use these products, and they're willing to pay to keep you addicted!

Next, recognize that quitting caffeine will require a significant effort on your part. However, unlike people who try to give up caffeine without nutritional support, you've got nutritious, energy-filled green juices on your side. It's likely that your withdrawal symptoms will start within a few hours of your usual caffeine fix, and some symptoms – particularly cravings – will probably last for as long as two to three weeks.

These symptoms include:

- Headaches
- Fatigue
- Decreased motor skills
- Difficulty concentrating
- Flu-like symptoms such as stuffy nose and cough.

In addition to increasing your intake of green juices during your caffeine detox, include some green tea in your daily plan. You can even chill green tea and mix it in with your juices. It contains mild traces of caffeine, and it is full of antioxidants. You can also enjoy herbal teas during this time and in the future. Like vegetables and fruits, these teas can contain traces of pesticide and herbicide if they are not organic – so choose organic teas, and begin enjoying better health without loading your system with caffeine and other toxins.

Finally, be sure to drink plenty of water now and into the future. Water helps your kidneys function properly, it helps to flush toxins from your system, and it can help to alleviate the symptoms of caffeine withdrawal.

Give yourself plenty of time for rest and relaxation, and continually remind yourself of the reasons you decided to eliminate caffeine from your diet. Keep drinking those juices, and soon you'll forget that you ever relied on caffeine for energy. As an added bonus, the money you'll save on those beverages will make it easier than ever to afford amazing green juices.

Here are some green juice recipes that are full of chlorophyll and B vitamins you can try in place of coffee to boost your energy to the sky and beyond!

Chlorophyll Instead of Coffee Green Juice

1 large cucumber
8 stalks of organic celery
1 handful of kale
1 handful of spinach
1 handful of parsley
1 handful of Swiss Chard
¼ lemon
1-inch piece of ginger

Juice all ingredients and consume first thing in the morning or before a workout.

Sun-Kissed Morning

    2 Oranges, peeled
    2 Carrots
    4 Swiss chard leaves
    1 Beet, peeled and quartered
    1 Inch ginger root (optional)

Juice all ingredients. Pour in a glass and enjoy immediately.

Sweet n' Sour Energy Juice

    ½ Fresh pineapple
    1 Handful spinach
    1 Grapefruit

Juice all ingredients. Pour into a glass over ice and enjoy.

Broccoli Power Blend

    ½ Head fresh broccoli, cut into large florets
    2 Stalks celery, with long fibers removed
    1 Carrot
    2 Oranges, peeled

Juice all ingredients. Pour into a glass and enjoy on its own or over ice.

Morning Glow Carrot-Pepper Juice

    2 Green bell peppers, seeds and stems removed
    2 Small cucumbers
    2 Lemons, peeled
    4 Carrots

Juice all ingredients. Pour into a glass and enjoy, either as is, or over ice.

Morning Glory Green Juice

5 Kale leaves

3 Romaine lettuce leaves

1 Handful spinach

2 Celery stalks, long fibers removed

1 green or yellow apple

1 Lemon, peeled

1 Cucumber

Juice all ingredients. This lovely light green juice tastes fantastic over ice.

Super Green Power Elixer

4 Kale leaves

1 Large cucumber

2 Pears

2 Celery stalks, long fibers removed

Juice all ingredients. This lightly sweet juice is lovely alone or over ice.

Olympian Power Blend

2 Beets, peeled and quartered

2 Large carrots

2 Celery stalks, long fibers removed

1 Orange, peeled

1 Tangerine, peeled

1 Handful baby bok choy or other greens

Juice all ingredients. This nutritious juice tastes great over ice.

Apple-Asian Pear Energy Blend

2 Asian pears

2 Tart apples (Granny Smith works well here)

3 Celery stalks, long fibers removed

1 Lemon, peeled

1 Handful baby spinach

Juice all ingredients and pour over ice. This light green juice tastes wonderful and is great for first-time juicers.

Super Cool Power Greenie

2 Pears

1 Handful spinach

1 Handful kale

1 Zucchini

1 Small cucumber

1/2 Lemon, peeled

1 Inch ginger root

Juice all ingredients, then enjoy over ice.

Fennel-Apple Pear Punch

2 Pears

1 Apple

1 Fennel bulb with green tops

Juice all ingredients, then enjoy over ice. This lightly licorice-flavored beverage has a sophisticated taste and a lovely color.

Green Juicing
to Boost Brain Power

If you only knew how much more alert, attentive and relaxed your brain could be on a regular basis with green juicing, you'd start and never stop. You'll find out just why green juicing is the ultimate brain boosting practice.

Our brains are a complex collection of neural pathways that run on several nutrients that are found readily in green juices. You don't have to suffer from dementia, Alzheimer's, or Lou Gehrig's disease as you get older, and you don't have to suffer from ADHD, ADD, loss of memory, a foggy brain, loss of concentration or poor cognition while enjoying your younger years.

Let's talk about how green juices really help to keep those neurons firing!

Green juices are like mini blood transfusions. They clear the cobwebs from the mind, quite literally. While leafy greens should still be the primary food in your green juices, things like apples or lemons also help to boost brainpower. This is because apples, for instance, have a chemical compound called **quercetin**. It is especially prevalent in red apples, and mostly in their skins. This chemical is a natural way to treat fragile capillaries but it also has anti-inflammatory, anti-viral, antioxidant, anti-allergy, and immune-modulatory properties.

This is all good news for your body as a whole and especially how your brain functions. Since apples are often used to 'sweeten' your green juices, and are often easy to come by organically, they are a wonderful way to keep your green juices both great tasting and incredibly healthy! This chemical in apples, quercetin, is also a flavanoid, which is a polyphenolic compound known to cure all kinds of diseases, but are especially beneficial to the brain and its overall functioning. It has even been proven to aid with Alzheimer's treatment at Cornell University.

Green juicing can also support brain health through the massive amount of phytonutrients, essential amino acids and other vitamins present in a liquefied, easily accessible form to the body and therefore to the brain. The more nutrients the brain has, the easier it can facilitate communication to all the organs of the body and also amongst the neurons of the brain.

Vitamin E is another essential nutrient for boosting brainpower. Luckily, there are many vegetables that contain plenty of Vitamin E – and any of these make great additions to green juices.

- Lettuce, all types
- Spinach
- Kale
- Collard Greens
- Mustard Greens
- Turnip Greens
- Cabbage
- Broccoli
- Green Beans
- Sweet Potatoes
- Summer Squash
- Zucchini
- Beets

Now take into consideration the fact that nutritional guidelines call for adults to eat just 2 ½ cups of vegetables daily. If you've already begun preparing green juices, you'll feel as though that's not much, and you're definitely right in your thinking – it really is not much at all. When you think about how many vegetables go into just a single green juice, you'll quickly realize that you're getting much more in terms of nutrition than the average person gets. All these extra vegetables translate into extra vitamins, which in turn power your brain and help keep you thinking clearly.

Nutrition experts also recommend that adults consume two cups of fruit per day. An apple is about one cup of fruit, and a pear is another cup. That's it. Fruits, like vegetables, contain vital nutrients that help to keep the brain humming along. Consider how much you'd be taking in if you enjoyed one green juice per day, then think about how much higher your nutritional intake would be with the addition of a second juice and maybe even a third. That's a lot of brainpower!

Besides helping you think clearly, all those fruits and vegetables help your brain in other ways:

- ⮑ Fruits and vegetables are rich in antioxidants. These vital nutrients help to preserve brain function by protecting tissue from damage caused by aging. High fruit and vegetable intake is directly linked to sharp cognitive skills.

- ⮑ Fruits and vegetables contain fiber that reduces the risk of stroke. Taking in plenty of fiber can help to reduce cholesterol, which in turn helps to prevent stroke. The type of fiber that clears the blood of cholesterol is the same kind found in green juices – soluble fiber.

- ⮑ Fruits and Vegetables help the brain stay flexible, thanks to the many vitamins they contain. Vitamin A, for example, is directly linked to improved learning capacity. Whether you need to learn a new skill, or if you're simply working to stay sharp as you grow older, Vitamin A will help you maintain your mental capacity.

- ⮑ Fruits and Vegetables contain plenty of ascorbic Acid, or Vitamin C. This water-soluble compound helps the brain to produce norepinephrine, which is a manor neurotransmitter that helps to regulate thinking. It also transports fats into the neuronal mitochondria, which are like the engines that help your brain cells work. Without it, the brain is not able to access the energy it needs. No wonder you feel foggy when you don't get proper nutrition!

By drinking just one green juice daily, you can help your brain function improve. By drinking two or more green juices, you can really give yourself a boost. Next time you're tempted to reach for a junk-food type snack, consider how it might affect you; then compare it with a green juice. I'm willing to bet you'll choose the juice, now that you know how it can help not just your body, but your mind to function at an optimal level.

Here are ten recipes for juices that will help you clear the cobwebs from your mind and enjoy greater brainpower.

Red, Blue, and Green
      2 Cups Watermelon, cubed
      6 Kale leaves or 1 handful spinach
      1 Cup blueberries

Juice all ingredients. Enjoy alone or pour over ice.

Purple Power Punch

>   5 Cups purple or black grapes
>
>   ½ Cup blackberries
>
>   1 Apple
>
>   1 Handful Bibb lettuce leaves

Juice all ingredients. Enjoy alone or pour over ice.

Peachy Keen Green Machine

>   2 Yellow summer squash, stems removed
>
>   6 Kale leaves
>
>   4 Small peaches, pits removed
>
>   1 Apple
>
>   ½ Lemon, peeled

Juice all ingredients. Enjoy alone or pour over ice.

Minty-Fresh Mind Booster

>   2 Kiwi fruits, peeled
>
>   2 Cups blackberries
>
>   15 Strawberries
>
>   2 Cups mint leaves

Juice all ingredients. Enjoy alone or pour over ice for a cool, sweet, refreshing treat.

Melon Madness

>   1 Apple
>
>   1 Pear
>
>   ½ Cantaloupe, seeded
>
>   ½ Honeydew melon, seeded
>
>   1 Handful baby spinach

Juice all ingredients. Enjoy alone or pour over ice.

Pure Green Mind Power

6 Kale leaves

2 Cups spinach

1 Small cucumber

3 Stalks celery, long fibers removed

2 Green Apples

1 Inch Ginger root

Juice all ingredients. Enjoy alone or pour over ice.

Pear-a-Green Falcon

1 Cup green grapes

1 Ripe pear

2 Cucumbers

1 Lime, peeled

Juice all ingredients. Enjoy alone or pour over ice. Soon, you'll be soaring like a falcon!

Feeling Great Greenie

2 Cups spinach

2 Green apples

6 Leaves Swiss chard

4 Celery stalks, long fibers removed

1 Small cucumber

1 Bunch Basil

Juice all ingredients. Enjoy alone or pour over ice.

Cranberry-Citrus Power Punch

1 Cup cranberries

1 Sweet apple

1 Cup cubed winter squash (butternut or acorn works well)

6 Collard leaves

1 Orange, peeled

Juice all ingredients. Enjoy alone or pour over ice.

Melon-Cucumber Crush

1 Cucumber
1 Lime, peeled
1 Cup honeydew melon, cubed
1 Kiwi fruit, skinned

Juice all ingredients. Enjoy alone or pour over ice.

Adding an Extra Kick to Your Green Juices: It's Easy!

Here you will learn how to add some interesting and easily available extra ingredients to your green juices and smoothies to make them even more amazing and nutrition-packed.

Let's get right to it—with some supplements you can add to your green juices to boost brainpower, heal the body and increase energy.

- ⮑ Put some spice into your life with cayenne pepper. This is a wonderful supplement to add to your green juices. It does all kinds of good things for your organs including the brain. It also stops bleeding intestines, dissolves blood clots, increases circulation to the head to reduce the chances of aneurism or stroke. Just 1/8 of a teaspoon (of 1500,00 heat units) added to your green juices can help prevent Alzheimer's disease, and senility and improve mental clarity. Cayenne is actually more beneficial when done with green juicing since taking cayenne pepper alone can cause intense stomach cramps or digestive discomfort.

- ⮑ Add some algae to your green juices. There are four major types of algae – spirulina, Chlorella, blue green algae, and Dunaliella (red algae). Most people in civilized nations consume way too much protein – and it is very hard for the body to break it down. What they really need are the amino acids in the proteins, and algae has a very high utilization percentage – which means your body can use up to 60-70% of it without having to work so hard to absorb it. You can use just ½ teaspoon in your juices daily to get algae's great benefits. Algae powder is the best thing to add to your juices, and actually is preferable over taking algae tablets because they are harder to digest. Just one type of algae – the blue green variety is a known brain booster. It is rich in neuropeptide precursors. These are important for the neurotransmitters in the brain to communicate with one another. It makes for better learning and memory as well as improving our abilities to adapt to changes in our environment – otherwise known as stress! The improved functioning of these neuropeptides also means that your pineal gland, an important endocrine gland in the center of the brain functions better. Many call it the 'master' gland of the body.

- Put a little nutritional yeast (Saccharomyces cerevisiae) in your green juices to prevent and aid: dementia, Alzheimer's disease, nervous system disorders, Multiple Sclerosis, premature senility, schizophrenia, Tourette's syndrome, neurological disorders, anxiety, depression, and emotional weakness. The reason nutritional yeast is such a great additive for your green juices is because it is full of B vitamins, which the nervous system and brain require to function at their best. One word of caution, however, if you have gout or the tendency to develop gout, don't use this supplement because the high protein levels can aggravate this disease. You can start with just two TBS per green juice – and add to just about every recipe presented in this guide.

- Barley or wheat grass is a great addition to your green juices. Because of their incredibly high nutrient content, added with your leafy greens and highly alkalizing green vegetables, barley and wheat grass take your green juices to the next level – they are literally food for your brain, so you will feel energized, mentally clear and full of life every day. Just add a few freshly juiced greens if you have the right kind of juicer (just a shot glass full is sufficient to add to any green juice) or use a few tablespoons of wheat grass or barley powder if you aren't juicing fresh.

- Organic, unfiltered apple cider vinegar with the "mother" is also a wonderful way to boost brain power. It also removes calcium deposits form the body so it can treat joints and muscles too. It also balances the body's pH levels, which the brain requires for its best performance. You can start with just 1 tablespoon per green juice you consume and add more as you desire over time.

There are of course other supplement you can add to your green juices – super food powders, and herbs, just to name a few, but these are a few great ones to start with and they are often easily found at health food stores or your local market. Green juicing is already amazing on its own, but if you want the Ferrari of green juices – these supplements will take your juicing habit to the next level.

Taking Your Juices to the Next Level with Super Foods

Perhaps you've heard of goji berries or acai, and you may have heard about maca root powder. If you think you've never heard of cacao, think again; this powerful super food is what gives chocolate its enticing flavor! In this chapter, you'll learn about many super foods you can add to your juices and blends to kick your body into stratospheric levels of health and wellness, plus you'll learn more about why some really common fruits and vegetables are considered to be super foods.

Super Foods are so named because of their high nutrient content, and because they contain important phytochemicals that are capable of increasing health and wellbeing. Many super foods have already made their way onto our lists: Spinach, blueberries, beets, and sweet potatoes are just a few examples of common super foods. Besides these more common ones, there are hundreds of others, which can be added to your green juices. To get the best benefits, look for super foods with high ORAC values.

What is an ORAC Value?

ORAC is an acronym that stands for *Oxygen radical Absorbance Capacity*. In a nutshell, an ORAC value is a way to measure a food's level of antioxidants. Foods that rank higher on the ORAC scale have high levels of antioxidants, so these foods are best for neutralizing the free radicals that can harm the body at a cellular level. Eating plenty of super foods with high ORAC values is an excellent way to help keep you looking and feeling youthful while eliminating damage that contributes to disease and age-related degenerative processes. Health experts recommend that people consume at least 3,000 to 5,000 ORAC units daily; without juicing, you can see how that might be a stretch when the downfalls of the modern diet are considered.

The Health Benefits of Super Foods

The health benefits of super foods are numerous. Eating plenty of these foods on a regular basis – and drinking them in your juice – can do more than simply protect you from rapid aging. Here are some ways adding super foods to your diet will benefit your health:

- ➲ Super foods reduce the risk of chronic disease developing
- ➲ Eating super foods as a major part of the diet may prolong healthy lifespan
- ➲ People who consume lots of super foods are generally less prone to obesity than those who do not

Top Ten Common Superfoods for Juicing

Ten top superfoods to consider include the following. The ORAC values listed are for 100 grams of the food, which comes out to about 3.5 ounces.

1. Beets – These vibrant root vegetables are known to help decrease hypertension, which is just one reason to include them in your green juices. They also contain loads of vitamins and minerals, and they have an ORAC score of 841.

2. Blueberries – With an ORAC value of 2,400. blueberries are powerful as well as tasty. They contain antioxidants that may reduce the risk of cancer.

3. Blackberries – These delicious berries contain lots of fiber, vitamins, minerals, and antioxidants. They come in just behind blueberries with an ORAC value of 2,036.

4. Broccoli – When your mother urged you to eat lots of broccoli, I hope you listened! This super food contains an abundance of vitamins and minerals; in addition, it has an ORAC value of 890.

5. Kale – In case you're wondering why kale is such a popular ingredient in green juices, it's not just because this leafy green is wonderfully nutritious in a variety of ways. Kale is the most powerful green in another way: It has an ORAC value of 1,770.

6. Raspberries – Raspberries are wonderfully flavorful, and they contain loads of vitamins as well as plenty of heart-healthy fiber. Raspberries have an ORAC value of 1,220.

7. Red Bell Pepper – Not too sweet, and very light tasting, red bell pepper contains high levels of vitamin C as well as lots of vitamin A. It is also filled with antioxidants, which give it an ORAC score of 713.

8. Spinach – If you prefer the taste of spinach over the flavor of kale, don't worry. Spinach is great for you, and it scores high with an ORAC value of 1,260.

9. Strawberries – Red, ripe, strawberries have an ORAC value of 1,540. They also contain lots of vitamin C and fiber, plus they're a low-calorie choice with plenty of flavor to add to green juices.

10. Tomatoes – Ripe, red tomatoes contain lycopene, which is an antioxidant that is less abundant in other foods. They also contain plenty of fiber, potassium, and vitamin C. Tomatoes have an ORAC value of 189. The more you enjoy, the higher that number will be.

Super Food Supplements

Not only can you enjoy everyday fruits and vegetables and benefit from their superb nutrition, you can also add a powerful antioxidant boost to green juices while adding exceptional flavor, just by stirring in a small amount of one of these supplements. Here's a list of 15 outstanding super food supplements and their approximate ORAC value per 100 grams (the oxygen free radical absorption capacity):

Food	ORAC Value
1. Sumac	312,400
2. Ground Cloves	290,283
3. Sorghum Bran	240,000
4. Dried Oregano	175,295
5. Dried Rosemary	165,280

6.	Dried Thyme	157,290
7.	Ground Cinnamon	131,420
8.	Ground Turmeric	127,068
9.	Dried & Ground Vanilla	122,400
10.	Ground Sage 1	19,200
11.	Szechuan Peppers	118,500
12.	Acai Powder	102,700
13.	Maca Root Powder	90,500
14.	Cocoa Powder	55,653
15.	Fresh Thyme	27,426

Adding Superfoods to Green Juices

As you can see, most of these superfoods are powders and as such, they don't contain any juice. Each of these superfoods also has a distinct flavor; for example, cocoa powder provides a taste of chocolate, while dried, ground vanilla provides the famous vanilla flavor so many people love. Szechuan peppers are very spicy, while many other superfoods; including thyme, sage, and oregano have distinctive herbal flavors.

If you'd like to add one or more of these ingredients to a green juice, the best way to do it is to prepare the juice first, pour it into a glass, then sprinkle the super food onto it. Some other super foods you can add this way include spirulina, kelp, and even certain essential oils, all of which add flavor and potent nutritional power to the juice you're drinking.

If you decide you want to try adding some essential oils to your juices, you'll love the flavor they add, and your body will appreciate the powerful healing boost they provide.

Here are a few of the best essential oils you can add to finished juices, along with their ORAC values:

- Clove Essential Oil – This is powerful stuff. It adds a hot, spicy, slightly sweet flavor to juices (try it with apple, pears, and spinach!) plus it has the biggest ORAC number or any essential oil: 1,078,700. Use just one drop at a time and be sure you're getting pure therapeutic grade essential oil to reap the benefits.

- Peppermint Essential Oil – Not only does peppermint essential oil help to freshen the breath, it also helps keep appetite in check while increasing mental clarity and promoting alertness. Peppermint essential oil has an ORAC value of 137,300.

- Lemon Essential Oil – When fresh lemons are hard to come by and you want to add a nutritional boost plus a zippy flavor to your juice, try a drop of lemon essential oil. Its ORAC value is 660.

- These are just a few of the many essential oils that are suitable for ingestion. When using them in juices, just add between one and two drops to the juice in your glass. Each drop contains the essence of a huge amount of the plant it is made with; for example, it takes 28 cups of mint to make one drop of peppermint essential oil.

Green Juicing FAQ's

We'll cover some of the most commonly asked questions, so you will be an expert.

1. Do I have to follow recipes exactly?

   Answer: No! You can make substitutions as you see fit. I encourage you to try new things and modify these recipes. Just changing one ingredient can make a big difference.

2. I have heard good things about juice fasts. Should I try one?

   Answer: This is totally up to you. I have conducted juice fasts and had excellent results; I've also heard from people who could not tolerate the extreme detoxifying effects juice fasting can cause. If want to try a juice fast, start with a short one and then work toward a longer one. If you have health conditions such as diabetes or hypertension, be sure to speak with your doctor about whether juice fasting is safe for you.

3. I am worried that juicing is going to take a lot of time. Can I do anything to make the process faster?

   Answer: Absolutely. Prepare your fruits and vegetables ahead of time and store them in the refrigerator. If you've cut any vegetables or fruit into pieces, be sure to use these items up within 24 hours since nutrients start to decrease once the protective skin is removed from the produce.

4. I want to have fresh juice at work, but there's no way I can bring my juicer to the office. Is there a solution?

    Answer: Yes. You can make a juice ahead of time and store it in a tightly sealed container in the refrigerator. It does lose some of its nutrients over even a few hours, so be sure to enjoy it before the end of the workday.

5. What is the maximum amount of time I can keep my juice fresh in the refrigerator? I just can't juice more than once a day or so.

    Answer: Juice keeps well for up to 72 hours. After that, it's basically ruined. Do try to make most of your juices right before drinking them, or drink within about 12 hours of making them. If you want to store juices for an extended period of time, place them in sealed containers with air space and freeze them. You can even make popsicles if you like. Just be sure to use frozen juices within 7-10 days to prevent nutrient loss.

6. Are there any fruits or vegetables I don't have to wash before juicing?

    Answer: No, all fruits and vegetables ought to be thoroughly cleaned before juicing, even if they are organic. Since these are raw juices, any bacteria from handling, storage, transportation, or even natural fertilizers used in growing could make their way into your juice and cause severe illness.

7. My juicer has different speeds. Which speed is best for soft fruits?

    Answer: In general, low speed is best for soft fruits, while high speed handles hard fruits and vegetables with ease. Always refer to your juicer's users' manual if you're stuck.

8. I feel like I am wasting a lot of juice because my pulp is still soaking wet. Is there some way I can recycle this?

    Answer: Absolutely. Scoop the pulp from its reservoir and put it into a pitcher or similar container you can use to feed it back into the juicer's intake chute. Re-juicing your pulp will help you to get the most from your produce.

9. I really like the taste of lemons and I love lemon zest. Can I juice lemons and other citrus whole, without peeling them first?

    Answer: If you have organic citrus fruits that have been well-washed, and if you have a juicer that's capable of handling tough items, go ahead and give this a try. There are many phytonutrients in citrus skin and though some feel this method produces bitter juice, others really like it.

10. I am traveling and I can't bring my juicer with me. Is there some other way I can keep incorporating fresh green juices into my daily diet?

Answer: If you're going on a short trip, consider freezing juices and packing them into a cooler with ice. Drink them as they thaw. If you cannot bring your own beverages (for instance, if you're flying,) look for a raw juice bar where you can order the same fresh green juices you make at home. Be prepared to pay top dollar for good juices; at the same time, be prepared to keep feeling great and return home with no guilt over having made poor nutritional choices while on holiday.

Your Super Encyclopedia Of Greens

In this chapter you will enjoy an alphabetized master list of greens, fruits, vegetables, and even additional mix-ins that can add some wonderfully surprising health benefits to your body. Think of this chapter as your encyclopedia of green juicing. You'll end up knowing all the health benefits of each ingredient as well as how they taste, what exactly is in them, and why they work, whether they are a protein, vitamin, mineral or other compound which is really great for your body. You'll also learn about possible side effects (though they are minimal) and any ingredients you should avoid, and why.

You can use this section of the guide as a reference while you are learning to make your own green juices, and over time, you will probably become a green juicing aficionado, knowing which things to juice when and why, without having to even look at these pages!

Name of Green	Health Benefits	Vitamins Minerals Nutrients	Taste	Possible Side Effects
Alfalfa	Used by the Chinese since the 6th century to aid numerous ailments, it cures kidney problems, reduces fluid retention and swelling, supports glandular functioning, lowers cholesterol levels, prevents strokes, relieves auto-immune disorders, cleanses the blood, bowels and liver, nourishes the digestive system and is one of the best land-based sources of trace minerals. In Arabic, it is called the 'Father of Plants" since its roots go deep into the earth to draw up nutrients form the soil.	B1, B6, C, E, K, trace minerals calcium, magnesium, phosphorous, iron, potassium	Earthy and moist	As with any herbal remedy, you have to be careful not to overdo it. If too much Alfalfa is consumed, the red blood cells will break down, and an amino acid called canavanine can aggravate a disease called Lupus. This amino acid is usually only found in the seeds and sprouts, though not the mature leaves. This plant should be avoided if you are pregnant because canavanine can also disrupt hormonal cycles.

Name of Green	Health Benefits	Vitamins Minerals Nutrients	Taste	Possible Side Effects
Arugula also known as rocket, roquette, rugula and rucola.	Arugula is an aromatic salad green. It is a cruciferous vegetable. Cruciferous vegetables are associated with reduced risk of cancer in many studies. Arugula is rich with valuable antioxidants, considered essential in preventing free radical activity in the body. Studies show that vitamin A and flavonoid compounds in arugula may help protect the body from skin cancer, lung cancer and oral cancer. Arugula is also a rich source of phyto-chemicals like sulforaphane, which has excellent chemoprotective effects and helps to fight carcinogens. Furthermore, Arugula is a good source of carotenoids, fat-soluble pigments that are known to help prevent macular degeneration. The vitamin C in arugula may help in the prevention of cataracts but it is also a powerful antioxidant that helps prevent cancer, boosts the immune system and fights the common cold. Vitamin A is a powerful antioxidant, boosts immunity and is great for the eyes, skin, bones and teeth. Arugula also provides 100% of the daily need for vitamin K with just three cups. Vitamin K is known to promote bone health and brain function while acting as an anti-inflammatory and antioxidant. Arugula supports weight loss. Due to its extremely low calorie content, while being packed with nutrients. Arugula supports bone health with low oxalate levels, and high vitamin K levels. Additionally, calcium, potassium, magnesium, manganese and vitamin C are all considered good contributors to positive bone health.	C, K and A. In addition to fighting free radical activity, these vitamins offer great immune system support. Arugula is also a good source of calcium, iron, potassium, manganese and phosphorous, all essential minerals. Low in Oxalate Oxalates inhibit mineral absorption in the body. Other healthy leafy greens, such as spinach, have high levels of oxalate. However, arugula appears to offer relatively low levels of oxalate, making it a healthier alternative for people seeking foods high in calcium and other essential minerals.	Tangy, Zesty	Arugula has no side effects

Name of Green	Health Benefits	Vitamins Minerals Nutrients	Taste	Possible Side Effects
Basil	Basil, a popular herb is used around the world. In addition to its versatile flavor, basil offers many health benefits. One of the primary medicinal uses for basil is for its anti-inflammatory properties. This effect stems from eugenol, a volatile oil in basil that blocks enzymes in the body that cause swelling, making basil an ideal treatment for people with arthritis. Basil, especially as an extract or oil, is known to have exceptionally powerful antioxidant properties that can arm the body against premature aging, common skin issues, age-related problems and even some types of cancer. Basil is also full of flavonoids orientin and vicenin, plant pigments that shield your cell structures from oxygen and radiation damage. Both fresh basil and basil oil have strong antibacterial capabilities. In fact, basil has proven to stop the growth of many bacteria, even those resistant to other antibiotics. Basil can be applied to wounds to help prevent bacterial infections. Also, by adding basil oil to your salad dressings, you can help ensure your vegetables are safe to eat. Basil oil can be used to treat constipation, stomach cramps and indigestion as well as the cold, flu, asthma, whooping cough, bronchitis and sinus infections. It is also a great source of magnesium, an essential mineral that helps the body's blood vessels relax, which can improve blood flow.	A, C, K, dietary fiber, manganese, magnesium, potassium	A fresh basil leaf eaten directly from the plant has an initial subtle peppery flavor. It then evolves into a slightly sweet flavor with a delicate menthol aroma.	There are no side effects for basil.

Name of Green	Health Benefits	Vitamins Minerals Nutrients	Taste	Possible Side Effects
Beet Greens & Stems	Because beet greens and stems are high in vitamin C, providving 30% of your total daily allowance in one serving, they act as a coenzyme to help synthesize certain amino acids. Due to high vitamin C levels, they also help the body produce collagen, a protein that supports healthy skin, bones, teeth and blood vessels. Your immune system also needs vitamin C to make white blood cells, which fight off infections. About 90 percent of vitamin C in the American diet comes from fruits and vegetables, such as beet greens. According to Nellie Hedstrom, nutrition specialist for the University of Maine Extension service. Your body uses fat to process and store vitamin A, which remains in your system longer than water soluble vitamins. Vitamin A is necessary for good vision, playing a role in light absorption in the rods and cones of your retina. You also need vitamin A for cell differentiation, immunity and healthy skin. Folate–Beet greens provide small levels of folate — about 2 1/2 percent of your daily value. Higher levels of folate exist in the bulb, about 17 percent of your daily value, so eat the whole plant, if possible. Folate functions in DNA synthesis, so has many important roles in your body such as preventing birth defects, making healthy blood cells and fighting cancer and heart disease. Folate is most well-known for preventing spinal defects in developing babies, and is therefore a vital nutrient for pregnant women.	Vitamins A, C, K, B6, E (Alpha Tocopherol), low in Saturated Fat and Cholesterol. High in Protein, Folate, Iron, Zinc, Pantothenic Acid, Phosphorus and a great source of Dietary Fiber, Thiamin, Riboflavin, Calcium, Magnesium, Potassium, Copper and Manganese.	Earthy and Bitter	Beet Greens and stems have no side effects, but they may cause stomach upset due to their bitterness if not used in moderation.

Name of Green	Health Benefits	Vitamins Minerals Nutrients	Taste	Possible Side Effects
Bok choy	Bok choy is a type of Chinese cabbage that doesn't look like a typical cabbage. It has dark green leaves connected to white stalks. One cup has just 9 calories and barely a trace of fat, yet delivers protein, dietary fiber and almost all the essential vitamins and minerals. Bok choy is a nutrient-dense food that offers several health benefits. It is also very low in calories.	Vitamins C, K, A, B-complex, anti-oxidants that are indicative of the Brassica family of plants–thiocyanates, indole-3-carbinol, lutein, zeaxanthin, sulforaphane and isothiocyanates, moderate source of minerals like calcium, phosphorous, potassium, manganese, iron and magnesium	Tastes like a cross between cabbage and lettuce, or perhaps spinach with a slight nutty flavor	There are no side effects to eating bok choy
Broccoli Leaves and Flowers	Used by the Romans, broccoli is considered a super-food due to its many nutrients. It is often called the crown jewel of nutrients. The US didn't cultivate broccoli until the 20th century but it was used long before that. Broccoli originated in Asia minor. Roman farmers called it 'the five green fingers of Jupiter.' It prevents cancer, maintains a healthy nervous system, regulates blood sugar levels, reduces cholesterol and helps with digestion due to its fiber content. Its high content of vitamin A is good for maintaining eyesight. Thanks to glucoraphanin, it also helps to repair skin cells.	A Brassica vegetable, it contains special antioxidants that occur specifically in this plant family: thiocyanates, indole-3-carbinol, lutein, zeaxanthin, sulforaphane and isothiocyanates, also Vitamins, A, B5, B1, B6, K, E, C, folic acid, fiber and calcium, iron, magnesium, potassium, manganese, and dietary fiber.	Tastes mild and earthy.	For those who are taking blood thinning medications, the excessive intake of broccoli is not a wise choice since it may interfere with the medications, thereby increasing the risk of stroke. Eating over one to two cups of broccoli a day may also increase the chances of dealing with kidney stones, so broccoli should be used sparingly in green juices.

Name of Green	Health Benefits	Vitamins Minerals Nutrients	Taste	Possible Side Effects
Endive, also known as Escarole	Endive is closely related to chicory. It is a cool-season crop native to Asia minor. It has curly narrow leaves as well as broad leaves. Current research studies suggest that high inulin and fiber content in escarole help reduce glucose and LDL cholesterol levels in diabetes and obese patients. It also helps to maintain healthy mucus membranes and skin. Its high content of vitamin A is good for maintaining eye-sight.	Vitamins C, A, Beta Cartoene, B-complex vitamins (B1, B3, B5, B6) good source of minerals like manganese, copper, iron, and potassium. Manganese is used as a co-factor for the antioxidant enzyme, superoxide dismutase. Potassium is an important intracellular electrolyte helps counter the hypertension effects of sodium.	Tangy and bitter-sweet taste.	Although this green leafy vegetable contains high concentrations of bitter glycosides and inulin, there are no known side effects when this vegetable is eaten in moderation.
Chard, also known as Swiss Chard	Swiss chard is packed full of good stuff. Recent research has shown that chard leaves contain at least 13 different polyphenol antioxidants, including kaempferol, the cardioprotective flavonoid that's also found in foods like broccoli and kale. It is also full of syringic acid, which is known for regulating blood sugar. It is a special flavanoid that is known to inhibit activity of an enzyme called alpha-glucosidase, which means fewer carbohydrates that we consume are broken down into simple sugars. This means a lesser incident of blood-sugar related illnesses like Diabetes. Chard also contains a beet like phytonutrients called betalain, which help with inflammation and free radical absorption. Chard also helps to support bone health with some of the highest levels of vitamin K–an amazing 716% DV is only exceeded by kale, spinach, and collard greens. Since it is full of iodine, chard also protects the thyroid.	Vitamins K1, A, C, E, B1, B2, B3, B5, B6, tryptophan, mangnesium, potassium, iron, manganese, copper, choline, calcium, phosphorous, folate, zinc, bioton, high iodine content	Strong, earthy taste	There are no known side effects of eating Swiss Chard, however, if you have an over-active thyroid, consult a doctor before consuming large quantities.

Name of Green	Health Benefits	Vitamins Minerals Nutrients	Taste	Possible Side Effects
Chickweed	A low-growing, soft plant often mistaken as a common weed. The whole plant is used to treat cuts, and also to relieve itching caused by eczema and psoriasis. It is also known to be good for rheumatism. It is demulcent (forms a soothing film over a mucous membrane, relieving minor pain and inflammation of the membrane). Mild alterative that corrects overall body imbalances. Taken internally, it helps soothe inflammation in the urinary system (eg. mild bladder infections, gastric and peptic ulcers). It also a good blood purifier by carrying away toxins. Internal use may also help to treat bronchitis, arthritis, and cold symptoms.	Rich in vitamin C, beta carotene, Vitamins B1, B2, and B3, Bio-flavonoids (including glycoside rutin) Coumarins, Omega 6 fatty acids, and trace minerals like copper, calcium, magnesium, manganese, iron, and silicon	Earthy , slightly bitter taste	No adverse effects.
Cilantro	One of the best benefits of cilantro is that it binds to heavy metal sin the body to help expel them as toxins. It has been used by naturopaths for centuries and was even considered a curative in Greek and Roman times. Cliantro reveres adverse effects of cardiovascular disease, can help cure diabetes, has anti-anxiety properties to calm your mood, improves sleep, lowers blood sugar levels, and has antibacterial, antifungal and antioxidant properties. Cilantro can also help lower 'bad' cholesterol. It has been used in Ayurvedic and Chinese medicine and is also a curative for poor digestion.	Rich in thiamin, zinc, dietary fiber and vitamins A, C, E and K. It has trace amounts of riboflavin, niacin, vitamin B6, folate, pantothenic acid, alcium, iron, magnesium, phosphorous, potassium, copper and manganese	Some call it 'soapy' in taste, but it is more like a mild mint or fresh tasting green	No known adverse effects of cilantro
Collard Greens	Collard greens help to improve bile production in the liver, lower bad cholesterol, offers a cancer-preventative in the form of 4 specific glucosinolates found in this cruciferous vegetable: glucoraphanin, sinigrin, gluconasturtiian, and glucotropaeolin. Collard greens help with overall detoxification of the body and have an anti-inflammatory effect as well. Collards are also very low in calories so they are a great green to add to juices if you are watching your weight.	Full of vitamins A, C, K, B1, B2, B3 B6, E, manganese, fiber, calcium, choline, tryptophan, iron, magnesium, folate, Omega 3s, potassium, and phosphorous	Strong, sometimes bitter and earthy taste	Aside from drinking too much too soon to cause a 'healing crisis' collard greens have no other adverse effects

Name of Green	Health Benefits	Vitamins Minerals Nutrients	Taste	Possible Side Effects
Dandelion Greens	Low in calories, dandelion greens have been shown to improve skin, hair and nails, reverse certain cancers, and greatly detox the body. The best part is you can often pick them from your own back yard since they grow as a common weed. They also contain more protein per serving than spinach, and dandelion greens contain all the essential amino acids, so it is a complete plant protein.	High in vitamins C, A and beta carotene, also full of calcium and iron, copper manganese, phosphorus, potassium, and magnesium. Dandelion greens also contain more calcium than kale.	Mild earthy taste	No known adverse effects
Dill	Native to Russia, the Mediterranean, and parts of Africa originally, this is a commonly grown herb all over the world now. Dill has two types of healing components: monoterpenes, including carvone, limonene, and anethofuran; and flavonoids, including kaempferol and vicenin. Dill also contains what are called 'volatile oils' (eugenol) act as a "chemo-protective" food (much like parsley) to help neutralize particular types of carcinogens, such as the benzopyrenes that are in cigarette smoke, charcoal grill smoke, and the smoke produced by trash incinerators. Dill helps to prevent bone loss, since it is full of calcium and important trace minerals that help the body absorb that mineral. Dill has the ability prevent bad bacteria from growing in the body through its high levels of antioxidants.	Dill is full of folic acid, riboflavin, niacin, vitamin A, C, beta carotene, and trace minerals like copper, potassium, calcium, manganese, iron, and magnesium	Soft, sweet taste	No known adverse effects

Name of Green	Health Benefits	Vitamins Minerals Nutrients	Taste	Possible Side Effects
Fennel	Fennel belongs to the Umbellifereae family and is therefore closely related to parsley, carrots, dill and coriander. Fennel has a unique combination of phytonutrients—including the flavonoids rutin, quercitin, and various kaempferol glycosides—that give it strong antioxidant powers. It also contains a 'volatile oil' called anethole, which has been known to cure certain cancers. It does this by shutting down intercellular signaling system called tumor necrosis factor (or TNF)-mediated signaling. Fennel also protects the colon, the heart and the overall health of the body. It can lower blood pressure and reduce free radicals in the body.	Vitamins C, some B3, folate, fiber, potassium, manganese, molybdenum, phosphorous, calcium, iron, copper, magnesium, phytonutrients	Crunchy and slightly sweet	No known adverse effects
Kale	Kale is low in calories and has no fat so it is the perfect food if you are reducing your calories. Kale supports cardiovascular health, prevents lung and oral cancers, it prevents bone loss, it also helps to detox the body due to high sulfur content.	More iron than beef, high in Vitamin K, A, C (ten times more than spinach), antioxidants, flavonoids, carotenoids, Omega 3s, calcium, fiber, sulfur	Often bitter due to high iron content, but you can't taste it in green juices	No known adverse effects
Miner's Lettuce	Sometimes confused with Purslane, Miner's Lettuce is picked from a trailing vine, and has tender, soft leaves. It has flourished in the wild for hundreds of years. Gold miner's used to eat it during the gold rush to keep their energy up. It grows all over California, but is also cultivated elsewhere.	Ascorbic acid (Vitamin C), A, iron, beta carotene, protein	Mild tasting	No known adverse effects
Mint	There are lots of varieties of mint. It was used traditionally in Indian and the Middle East and Asia. It is considered an aromatic. Mint soothes the digestive tract, and helps with a stomachache, as well as irritated bowel syndrome (IBS). It can help with skin disorders including acne, and helps to eliminate toxins from the body. Mint can also help to whiten the teeth and it also cleans the blood.	Rich in vitamin C and beta carotenes, also full of a good source of several essential minerals, including magnesium, copper, iron, potassium, and calcium	Sweet with a cool aftertaste	No known adverse effects

Name of Green	Health Benefits	Vitamins Minerals Nutrients	Taste	Possible Side Effects
Mustard Greens	A cruciferous vegetable, mustard greens are cholesterol lowering, also full of a chemical compound called glucosinolate which can help cure certain types of cancer. Mustard Greens are also anti-inflammatory.	Full of vitamins K, A, E, B1, B2, B3 B6, C, E, fiber, copper, magnesium, tryptophan, potassium, folate, phosphorous, and calcium	Slightly bitter	No known adverse effects
Parsley	Parsley is often thought of as a garnish but it is a great green juicing additive. It contains two types of volatile oil components—including myristicin, limonene, eugenol, and alpha-thujene. The second type is flavonoids—including apiin, apigenin, crisoeriol, and luteolin. Parsely is chemoprotective and can prevent tumors. It also contains luteolin, a flavanoid that helps to clean the blood.	Folic acid, Vitamins B, C	Earthy, mild taste, can be slightly peppery	No known adverse effects
Purslane	Purslane is native to India and has been spread throughout the world from its original cultivation there. It is considered a wild weed but is very nutritious. It grows prevalently since it requires less water and soil nutrients than many other plants. It is low in calories but high in many important vitamins, trace minerals and essential nutrients. Its high antioxidant levels (especially melatonin) help to prevent certain types of cancer, and promote heart health.	High in vitamin A, Omega 3s, C, B-complex vitamins, and two alkaloids, (betalain) Also full of trace minerals like calcium, copper, iron, magnesium, manganese, phosphorous, zinc, selenium, as well as folates	Mild, slightly sweet taste	No known adverse effects

Name of Green	Health Benefits	Vitamins Minerals Nutrients	Taste	Possible Side Effects
Raspberry Leaf Greens	Raspberry leaf greens have been used for centuries to make medicinal teas. The leaves contain a natural astringent that help to cleanse the body. Raspberry leaves are also known to improve fertility in women. They can also help to regulate hormonal changes that accompany menstruation. The leaves can also help to promote stronger reproductive organs and muscles. This plant also helps with constipation, poor blood circulation, inflammation, diarrhea, irritated skin, gum diseases, oral cavities, the cold and flu, respiratory infections, and other digestive issues.	Full of C, E, A, and B complex, minerals such as calcium, phosphorus, potassium, magnesium, iron and antioxidants.	Tender, sweet and tart	No known adverse effects
Radish Leaves	Radish leaves are full of more antioxidants and important nutrients than the radishes themselves. Radish leaves have been used to treat kidney and skin disease as well as cure certain types of cancer due to a high levels of a chemical compound called anthocyanins. The leaves can even be turned into a poultice to help with insect bites.	Iron, calcium, B-complex vitamins, vitamin C, protein, and zinc	Mild to extreme peppery flavor	No known adverse effects
Spinach Leaves	Spinach is a great green juice additive. It has anti-cancer qualities (especially with prostate cancer) and is full of a special plant nutrient called glycoglycerolipids, which are what help the plant in its process of photosynthesis but also supports the cells of humans.	High levels of phytonutrients such as carotenoids (beta-carotene, lutein, and zeaxanthin) and flavonoids, Vitamins K, A, C, E, B1, B2, B3, B6, manganese, iron, selenium, choline, copper, zinc, potassium, manganese, tryptofan, and folate	Mild taste	No known adverse effects

Name of Green	Health Benefits	Vitamins Minerals Nutrients	Taste	Possible Side Effects
Sunflower Sprouts	Sunflower sprouts have high concentrations of the mineral, zinc, which has been shown to improve sperm count in men. They also help support pregnant women due to high folate levels. Sunflower sprouts are a good source of plant-based protein, and are in fact considered to be one of the most complete sources since they contain all the essential amino acids. Sunflower sprouts boost the immune system and build the skeletal, muscular, and	High in folate, vitamins C, E, B, essential amino acids,	Mild taste	No known adverse effects

Get Your Free Bonus Below!

To get instant access to your free email course *"10 Days To Everlasting Health"* either click the link below if you are reading the digital version:

http://greensmoothies.me/freecourse

Or manually copy the URL directly to your Internet browser!

A Special Request From Elizabeth

Thank you so much for reading my book. I hope you really liked it! As you probably know, many people read through the different reviews on Amazon before they decide to purchase a book.

If you enjoyed reading my book and feel like you've got some great tips and information about smoothies, could you please take a minute to leave a review with your feedback?

60 seconds of your time is all I'm asking for, and it would mean the world to me.

Thanks For Your Help!

Elizabeth Swann

Elizabeth Swann (Miller) has over 10 years of experience as a practicing Naturopath (ND) specializing in healing through nutrition. She has degrees both in Psychology and Naturopathy.

As a person struggling with overweight throughout her childhood, teens and early 20's, Elizabeth decided to take charge, take stock and start making changes in her life for the better.

Her experiences with thousands of clients and her own personal experiences have led her to become an author. Her goal is to educate as many people as possible about the healing powers of food and how to easily incorporate these changes into daily life.

Elizabeth is happily married, has two beautiful daughters and currently lives and practices in Mount Carmel in sunny Israel.

Want to talk with Elizabeth? Email her at: Elizabethswannbooks@gmail.com
Or on her website: http://www.greensmoothies.me

9042663R00084

Printed in Great Britain
by Amazon.co.uk, Ltd.,
Marston Gate.